www.coolstuffmedia.com

San Clemente, CA

This book belongs to _____

Cover Design: Kent Healy
Art Director: Kent Healy
Graphic Design: Kent and Kyle Healy, Brian Bengelsdorf
Illustrator: Shawn King
Editor: Joe Tinervia
Consultant: Ted Savas

Cataloging-in-Publication Data is available from the Library of Congress.

First "Cool Stuff" edition, printed 2005
Second "Cool Stuff" edition, printed 2005
ISBN 0-9760258-0-9

Published by
"Cool Stuff" Media, Inc.
San Clemente, CA, USA

"Cool Stuff" titles are available at special discounts for bulk purchases in the United States by corporations, athletic teams, non-profits, and other organizations. Please contact us at www.coolstuffmedia.com, or e-mail us at sales@coolstuffmedia.com.

Waves...

... travel independently
across oceans, fearless,
focused, and free.

—Kent & Kyle Healy

I wish I had Cool Stuff they should teach in school when I was younger. It is a guaranteed blueprint for building a lifetime of fulfilling relationships, happiness, and financial success starting now!

— Jack Canfield
Co-author, *Chicken Soup for the Teenage Soul*
and *Chicken Soup for the College Soul*

Having the fundamentals promotes success in the surf and in life. Kent and Kyle's book offers a foundation to flourish in the real world. It's awesome. Get it!

— The Gudauskas Brothers
Ages 19, National Surfing Champions and scholar students

As a father of six children and grandfather of thirteen, I subscribe to the excellent and much-needed work of Kent and Kyle Healy. Even though I developed my own investment firm, my critical calling was to train my children to be responsible, productive, and basically happy adult members of our society. Your call to self-empowerment for young people tracks perfectly with what I have learned over many years. Good show!

— Jack Sullivan
Co-founder of Harris Bretall Sullivan & Smith Investment Firm,
San Francisco, California

The challenge of educators today is to provide the tools young people need outside of the classroom as well as within ... from how to relate well to peers, parents, and teachers to the ever-critical first job interview. Unfortunately, when push comes to shove, "real life" skills take a back seat to academics. Kent and Kyle have compiled much-needed words of wisdom for today's young adults! As their former teacher, I can attest to the fact that they have put their advice to use in their own lives. The result is two extremely successful young men who are willing to share their knowledge and expertise with others. This should be required reading for all young people!

— Michelle Bissonette
Teacher, Los Altos, California

I had really high expectations, and Kent and Kyle exceeded them! Well done, guys.

— Kevon Saber
Vice President of GenPlay Games and former President of AllDorm

Kent and Kyle have clearly hit the right tone and notes with respect to the DNA of life's common-sense approaches to success. Great reading not only for teens, but young adults of all walks and desires.

— Jim Smaha
Retired President, National Semiconductor Group,
National Semiconductor Corporation

This book should be required reading for all High School students before they graduate. Kent and Kyle Healy are extraordinary young men. They discovered early in life that basic principles about relationships, finances, goal setting, and much more were not taught in school. Any student or adult that reads this book will come away with a better plan for life.

— Dr. Michael McMurray
D.C., C.C.S.P., Chiropractor and lecturer

My daughter received your book as a gift. She loved it and gave 14 copies to her friends. Then I ordered fifty books for my office to help get the word out. This book has something for everyone. Well done!

— Lisa Wada

Mother and Businesswoman

This book is marvelous! Kent and Kyle Healy are great blokes who don't just write great keys to "cruising into the real world ... with styyyyle" - they live them!
It covers great practical topics and is a must for any teen - or any curious parent - who wants to learn how to thrive in THE REAL WORLD! 5 Stars - It's a must!

— Sam Humbert

Student, age 14, Australia

Firstly, I would like to commend the both of you for writing such an inspirational book. It's hard to find well-written, informative material that is centered toward people my age.

The book is especially unique in its composition. Few writers can relate to the teen audiences as well you guys have. The non-aggressiveness of your book combined with your entertaining stories and real life experiences will make "Cool Stuff" they should teach in school a sure winner among teens. You two have fully succeeded in winning my admiration, and without a doubt the esteem of other teens in the coming months.

The information that I have learned from this book has in several ways, changed my life. That's another thing you guys have hit gold on: writing suggestions and ideas that can easily be applied to anyone's life.

One example was the attitude chapter (which I really enjoyed). I learned that attitude is key, and the way you view life will affect how successful you become. The next day I decided to try what you said.

Miraculously, I began to see results immediately from the start. Not only did I seem to enjoy myself more than ever, but I could sense that people around me were drawn to my assuredness and optimistic attitude. Now I feel I am in more control of my life than ever before.

— Jim Suchy
Student, age 16

I am a senior at Santa Clara University and have done a lot of reading in my college career. I've read a lot of books, but it took picking up "Cool Stuff" to realize reading isn't always just homework—it can be enjoyable as well. I can honestly say that this is the first book I have ever read that I didn't "have" to read and I enjoyed every word of it. It's definitely a must read for anyone interested in anything!

— Sam Infantino
Student age 21

We started selling "Cool Stuff" in our stores and immediately noticed the results with our personnel—then we purchased copies for the rest of our staff! The perfect gift to give employees a jump-start on life. Attitude, goal setting, people skills, money management ... information everyone needs. Knowledge is power and contributes to a great work environment.

— John F. Merwald III
Cingular Wireless

MAKE IT HAPPEN!

This isn't a book, it's a movement.
— Dan Poynter, Author/Speaker

We're facing an epidemic! Each year millions of students graduate from our schools and a startling percentage are totally unprepared for the real world.

We need to work together to motivate and educate young people to not only survive, but also thrive outside of school. There are certain fundamentals that are necessary to win the game of life, but they are not being addressed in schools or at many homes today. We believe with the right tools, anyone can get the results they want in their life. Like Dan Poynter said, "This isn't just a book; it's a movement!" Let's work together and become part of the solution.

Please spread the word. You can make a difference.

Your mates, Kent & Kyle

I have never let
my schooling get
in the way of my
real education.

—attributed to
Mark Twain

"Cool Stuff"™ Media Inc

Dedication

Our parents encouraged us to ask questions and talk about life. We got used to hearing Dad say, "Isn't that just common sense?" The standard joke was:

"WHY IS IT CALLED 'COMMON SENSE' IF IT'S SO UNCOMMON?"

We found that what is often considered "common sense" really isn't so obvious. Our dad always—and we emphasize always—talks to us about people skills, basic financing, attitudes, goal setting, and how to recognize opportunities. Soon, these ideas were branded into our brains. We weren't always keen listeners, but now that we are older (and hopefully wiser), we're grateful he made the effort because:

"WE'RE NOT TAUGHT THESE SKILLS IN SCHOOL."

Not surprisingly, we dedicate this book to our parents for instilling in us the most priceless gift of all ... the belief that anything is possible when you put your mind to it. We also appreciate all the encouragement they've given us throughout our lives. Thanks so much!

Others, too, provided seemingly endless help and encouragement. We want to give a special and sincere "Thank you!" to those people (listed

in alphabetical order) for all their help in the production of this book and
their enthusiasm, advice, and amazing support:

Brian Bengelsdorf
Michelle Bissonette
Craig Bramscher
Jack Canfield
Mark DiRienzo
The Fusion Group: Lucy, Jennifer, Danielle, and Cheri
Mark Victor Hansen
Sue Hoffart
Shawn King
Mike and Barbara McMurray
Paul McWilliams
Dan Poynter
Ted Savas
Joe Tinervia
Linda Toth
Jamie Troughton
Anne Marie and Bernie Vogel
The Big Man Upstairs

"Thank you!" to all the other people who have certainly
helped us get to where we are now:

Dave Ahrens, RB Alexander, Gregg and Tucker Arth, Darrel Boyle,
Matt and Carlie Castle, Don Clelland and Diane Jones, Tom Davis, the
Foley Family, Art and Olga Frazer, the Haines Family, Tom Hermstad, Blake
Lund, Bruce Kennedy, Shannon McElyea, Bob Nealy, Dr. Linda Newell, Ted
Newland, Kevon Saber, Meghan Sandlin, John Sax, Jim Smaha, Peter
Solvik, Jack Sullivan, Jo Anne Thompson, Gary Ward, Jim and Kimberley
Wilson, our water polo teams, and all of our school friends.

And, of course, our thanks to all the businesses that helped
us gather facts and information.

EVALUATE YOURSELF

Thinking of putting down this book? Before you do, you might want to ask yourself...

>> Do you know what you want out of your life?

>> Do you always leave a good impression with your peers and adults?

>> Do you know specifically what employers are looking for when hiring?

>> Do you know how to start your own business and become your own boss?

>> Do you know how to handle your money and get it to work for you?

>> Do you know how to motivate yourself to reach your FULL potential?

>> Do you know how to get the life YOU WANT?

In this book, we will give you some extra momentum so you can live the life you want and deserve. If you promise to read and apply this information to your life, we promise you will see an improvement. Sound good? Let's go!

Table of Contents

SECTION FOUR:

SECTION FIVE:

HOW TO READ
THIS BOOK

We want you to get the most out of this book.
So, we have given you a bit of a head start by including tips and methods we used while doing all of our research.

Don't be shy... try these out:

>> Claim your book! Put your name in it, and make it yours.

>> Don't preserve your book for all of eternity. Get into it! Highlight topics and ideas that really stick out to you.

>> "Dog ear" your favorite pages by folding the top corners so you can refer back to them quickly and easily.

>> Read with an open mind, and be willing to accept and apply new information and ideas.

>> Use the space at the end of each chapter to jot down your thoughts and notes.

>> Keep your book handy so you can read it when you have a few extra minutes on your hands.

>> Don't read too much at once. There's a lot to take in. Think about what you have read before overloading your brain with more information.

>> Reread the areas you'd like to improve in.

INTRODUCTION

The genesis:

CREATING THE BOOK

After being on the planet almost 18 years, we realized almost all of the best stuff we've learned has been outside of school. We learned that garbage bags don't double as parachutes ... money doesn't grow on trees ... and attitude is important. We also learned how to surf on the beaches of New Zealand ... and that anyone — even a 16-year-old — can own their own business.

It turns out there is a whole lot of important and *"Cool Stuff"* out there that we need to know to survive in the real world. And — you guessed it — they don't teach it in school.

Why Did We Bother Writing This Book When We Could Have Been Surfing Instead?

How come we learn about French painters who died 300 years ago but not how to get along with others today? Why don't we learn how to make enough money to pay for a road trip or save the money once we get it?

Hardly rocket science! We're talking about how to get a job, make a buck (or a million), read the fine print, deal with adults, set goals to get what you want, control your moods, and even be your own boss. We wanted answers to our questions!

So where are we supposed to find out the things that we're not taught in school? We weren't about to open our own school, so we decided we'd start writing the book that NEEDED to be written!

Now let's get two things straight ...

>> One, WE SURE DON'T KNOW EVERYTHING!

>> Two, we don't pretend this book is an "encyclopedia of knowledge." (But we do think it's a good start.)

We still screw up. In fact, the biggest lesson we learned while putting this book together is "There is always more to learn." It's bad enough when you hear "You didn't know that!?" But it's even worse when you hear "You STILL don't know that!?" Here's your chance to avoid this.

We Wrote This Book Because ...

Looking back, we realized we lost a lot of good surf time. But we have no regrets! After all, we had good reasons for writing this book:

>> We wish we had a book like this.

>> We want to pass on the stuff we've learned (you may as well learn from our mistakes rather than your own).

>> We want to help others open their eyes to new concepts and provide some basic tools to help them build a promising future.

>> We want you to know it's possible for anyone to be extraordinary and fulfill their dreams.

>> We thought we'd save you some pain. We believe this book will make your life easier and far more fun.

Another Reason You Should Read This ...

"WE'RE TEENAGERS WRITING FOR TEENAGERS. WE'RE NOT SOME BORING FINANCIAL GUY, LAME PSYCHIATRIST, OR PARENT ON A POWER TRIP TRYING TO LECTURE YOU."

We certainly didn't write this book because we have galactic-sized intellects or supernatural powers. We have to admit, we thought it would be easy to sit down and write a book. WRONG! Another lesson learned:

"YOU HAVE TO BE SMART ENOUGH TO APPRECIATE HOW LITTLE YOU KNOW IN ORDER TO BECOME WISER."

We have done a huge amount of research. And we're talking HUGE. We've waded through waaaay too many boring manuals, motivational books, websites, booklets, and guides. We've conducted surveys, asked zillions of questions, and spoken with countless smart, successful, knowledgeable people.

We struggled to stay awake through seminars where old people rambled on about important (but really dull) stuff. Hundreds of hours later, we had sore brains and one heck of a lot of information. We have gathered the most interesting, essential bits and put them all in one place for you — here, in this book.

Take advantage of all of this information NOW! Eventually, you'll have to face many of the issues this book deals with. Why not get a head start and save yourself some grief? We did the footwork so you don't have to!

So read on, and get ready for real life. Remember: It's just a matter of being armed with the right information — and, of course, using it properly.

"AFTER ALL, WHY STUMBLE INTO THE REAL WORLD WHEN YOU CAN CRUISE IN ... WITH STYYYLE?!"

No Less Than
Success

01

What would you do
if you knew you
could not fail?

RRRIGHT
WHAT-EVERRRR

THE ONLY LIMITS TO YOUR POTENTIAL ARE THOSE YOU GIVE YOURSELF.

"Rrriiiiiigggght. What-everrrr." This is what we often heard when we told others that we were writing a book. Even some of our friends looked at us funny. Luckily, other people encouraged us. To be honest, it was kind of scary. We put in so much of our time, effort, and money without ever knowing if it would all pay off. But regardless of what might happen, we were determined to give it our best shot.

[Note: This is where we get to the inspirational bit. So quit yawning for a few minutes, and read on!]

DITCH
MEDIOCRITY

A HALF EFFORT IS AS CLOSE TO
THE BOTTOM AS IT IS TO THE TOP.

The first step to success is telling yourself you will not settle for anything less than the best you can do. Accepting mediocrity is easy—too easy. If you ditch mediocrity, you'll reach your potential much faster. Why would anyone be satisfied with anything but his or her best?

Usually it involves two reasons: They are either unmotivated or afraid of failure. If you relate to one or both of these, it's OK. There is still hope! We'll do our best to bail you out of these traps. Apply what you are about to learn to your life, and you're off and running. Deal? Let's go!

We all know it's easier to be lazy, not take the extra steps, just give in to mediocrity. The difficult part is getting the desire, the discipline, and the attitude necessary to succeed.

Most people prefer success, but few have the discipline to follow through and make it happen. You might be saying, "Well, duh, I know I need discipline, but how do I get it?" **Here's the first thing you need to know:**

DISCIPLINE COMES BY CONVINCING YOURSELF
THAT THE SACRIFICES ARE WORTH THE REWARDS.

There will be times when you don't feel like doing something (like maybe reading this book). This is when you must dig deep, keep all the rewards in mind, and finish what you have started. You'll soon see that this small effort will benefit you for the rest of your life.

It's time for a secret. Every successful person knows this, and now you do too:

"Cool Stuff"

"L U C K" IS SPELLED W-O-R-K.

It's a bummer, but it is true. If you rely on luck to run your life and wait for something good to happen, you will be about 90 years old before you realize most things worthwhile don't happen by chance. As someone once said, "The only thing that comes to us without effort is old age."

No one can share their discipline with you. They can only tell you how to get it. Those who have discipline acquire it because they realize the world does not owe them anything. They have discovered that if they want something out of life, they need to work for it. Most people don't truly understand this concept. They only want to see the results ... they expect success to just *happen* to them.

Unfortunately, it doesn't work this way. Expecting everything to just happen for us only guarantees dissatisfaction and disappointment, which is not what we want. That's why it's so important to see the direct connection between luck and work:

I FIND THAT THE HARDER I WORK, THE MORE LUCK I SEEM TO HAVE.

—*Thomas Jefferson*

To understand how work translates into luck, consider one of our friends. He always travels to exotic places such as Fiji, Indonesia, Hawaii, and Australia—all expenses paid. Wouldn't you say he is pretty lucky? Wouldn't you like to be in his shoes? Well, you're not the only one. Wherever he goes, people comment about how lucky he is.

But let's take a look behind the scenes. How did this guy land this lucky lifestyle? Well, he earned it. Since he was eleven years old, he woke up at five o'clock every morning to practice and become a better surfer. After six years of hard, disciplined training, he won a major surf competition where he was recognized by one of the largest companies in the industry and earned sponsorship. As a result, his efforts gave him the amazing opportunity to travel the world over—for free!

2K TIP

CLEAR IT. Don't dine and ditch. If you eat dinner at someone's house, always help clear the table. It shows you're not spoiled and you appreciated the grub. You can never go wrong by cleaning up or offering a helping hand. A great guest is always welcome.

This didn't happen overnight. He went six years without sleeping in, he sacrificed time with friends, and he balanced school and work too. Now does this sound like LUCK or more like W-O-R-K?

> *IT TOOK ME 16 HARD YEARS TO BE AN OVERNIGHT SUCCESS.*
>
> —Nick Nolte, Actor

THE COMFORT ZONE

Many people remain average or mediocre because they are too afraid to leave their comfort zones. This is the area where you feel safe and secure, a place to avoid embarrassment. Rarely traveling outside your comfort zone only slows down the learning process and in the end does not help you much. It's not always easy to leave this zone because it's a place where you're safe and feel risk-free.

You know how hard it can be to pull yourself out of that comfy chair in the family room and turn off the TV. But by taking chances, making mistakes, and learning from them, you'll help yourself excel. This is one of the best ways to meet your full potential and accomplish what you're truly capable of.

When we wrote this book, we had to step out of our comfort zone and explore the unknown. We'll always remember the day we came up with the idea. We looked at each other and shared an uncomfortable laugh. A book? How are we going to do that? Writing a book seemed waaay too hard. What if no one likes it? It was definitely out of our comfort zone. But by stepping out, we realized we were capable of more than we thought.

So think about it. If you don't expose yourself to failure, how are you going to make that team, buy that car, get straight A's, or ask that "special someone" on a date?

"Cool Stuff"

THERE IS ALWAYS A RISK OF FAILING WHEN YOU TRY SOMETHING, BUT BY NOT TRYING, YOU GUARANTEE FAILURE.

THE FEAR FACTOR

FEAR IS THAT LITTLE DARKROOM WHERE NEGATIVES ARE DEVELOPED.

—Michael Pritchard

Why do people get stuck in their comfort zones? Simple: fear. We easily could have let our fears imprison us a number of times in our lives. Fortunately, we did not allow our fear of rejection to hold us back.

> "Cool Stuff"
>
> FEAR IS JUST FOCUSING ON
> WHAT YOU DON'T WANT TO HAPPEN.

People have a tendency to focus on what they don't want. Instead, get your brain on your side, and clearly picture the way you want things to be. Ask yourself this question (and think hard about the answer):

> "Cool Stuff"
>
> WHAT WOULD YOU DO IF
> YOU KNEW YOU COULD NOT FAIL?

If no one would judge you and if you had nothing to lose, think of how you would approach things differently. We'll bet you would try all sorts of things if you knew you couldn't fail. Your answer is only the beginning of what you're really capable of doing. Once you recognize what you want from life and realize that failure only makes you a stronger, wiser person, you'll find that anything is possible. If you have the right mindset, you will soon see that failure is simply an opportunity for us to get ahead. It shouldn't be this huge barrier that holds us back. In fact, we need failure. [No, we haven't lost it! Just think about it.] If we don't expose ourselves to things that challenge us, we can't learn anything new. We'd never grow if that were the case.

What if Kelly Slater stopped surfing because he lost a surf competition? What if Julia Roberts quit acting because she did not get the first role she auditioned for? What if Thomas Edison gave up on the light bulb after thousands of unsuccessful attempts? (Yes, thousands!) Who knows what you and this world would miss out on if you let fear hold you back?

If you learn from your mistakes, failing can be just as important as succeeding. It's easy to be fooled into thinking success comes easy. It doesn't. Every accomplished person has failed many times along the way to get to where they are today.

LOOK AT THE BIG PICTURE.
FAILURE IS A PREREQUISITE TO SUCCESS.
YOU MAY LOSE ONE BATTLE,
BUT IF YOU STOP FIGHTING AND GIVE UP,
YOU'LL BE SURE TO LOSE THE WAR.

—Linda Toth

Door-to-door salesmen expect failure 90% of the time. They get turned down at least 9 out of 10 times before making a sale. They concentrate on the 10% that do buy. They realize they must visit 100 houses to make 10 sales. You're going to hear a lot of "no's" before you get your first "yes." It's just part of the process on the way to success.

When you don't get the result you want, look at it as an opportunity to learn something you didn't know before. Lift yourself up, and try again. If you know you can succeed and persist through your challenges, you won't fail.

"Cool Stuff"
FALLING DOWN ISN'T FAILING.
IT'S ONLY FAILING IF YOU STAY DOWN.

WHO ARE YOUR MATES?

Ask yourself, "Who are my friends?" They play a bigger role in your life than you think. Your friends influence your attitude, opinions, and the way you handle situations in your life. Whether you recognize it or not, you will rise or fall to their level. Take sports, for example. When a good team plays a better team, they usually rise up to the challenge and play

better. And when a good team plays a weaker team, they often play down to their level. We cannot emphasize this enough: Who you hang out with will affect your potential!

The friends you choose are a reflection of you. Spooky, huh? An old Jewish proverb states, "A person can look in the mirror, but if they really want to know themselves, they should look at the friends they choose." Try to find friends that challenge you to become a better person.

> **"Cool Stuff"**
>
> YOU CAN'T SOAR LIKE AN EAGLE
> WHEN YOU HANG WITH TURKEYS.

While attending different schools, we discovered an interesting concept about the impact of our friends on our performance. It doesn't take a genius to realize similarities between an individual and his friends. However, when we took a closer look, we found that people seemed to share the same level of achievement as their friends. In fact, the similarity was measurable in their grades.

We call it the "Cool Stuff" 5 Factor. Check it out yourself:

"Cool Stuff" 5 factor

Step 1: List five friends you spend the most time with. Then write their GPAs (grade point average) next to their names:

Friend 1: _____ GPA: _____

Friend 2: _____ GPA: _____

Friend 3: _____ GPA: _____

Friend 4: _____ GPA: _____

Friend 5: _____ GPA: _____

Step 2: Add all 5 GPA scores:

GPA 1 _____ + GPA 2 _____ + GPA 3 _____ +

GPA 4 _____ + GPA 5 _____ = _____

Step 3: Now divide the total by 5:

Total GPA _____ / 5 = Average GPA _____

Step 4: Enter your GPA here: _____

Step 5: Compare your GPA to the average GPA.

Note: Is the average GPA close to yours? If so, do you think your friends challenge you enough to succeed?

ARE YOU HUNGRY?

No, not that kind of hunger. We're talking about the hunger that makes your brain grow and not your gut. Do you feel you're being force-fed knowledge at school? If you can teach yourself to be "hungry" for knowledge, life will be easier and more fun. When you want to learn, you will be amazed at how little it takes to absorb and remember information. Scientists have found that exercising your brain improves its efficiency. With desire and exercise, it will only get easier and easier to become wiser and more successful. Eat up!

WHAT'S MISSING?

Wouldn't it be nice to be perfect? To have nothing wrong with you and always be ready to handle anything life throws at you? Too bad reality does not allow it. We all know no one is flawless. But this doesn't mean we can't strive to be better. No, you don't need to be "Ms. Perfect" or "Mr. Perfect." No, you don't need to act like you never do anything wrong, but you must certainly challenge yourself to become a better person. This means asking yourself, "What's missing? How can I improve?"

No one really likes to discover their faults and flaws, but those who do get an instant advantage. How? By finding their weaknesses and making them their strengths. Anyone who is successful knows there is always room for improvement. Develop a will for change, and always search for ways to become a better person.

GOT
DIRECTION?

One of the best methods for self-improvement is to get direction. Role models help you stay focused, stay motivated, and achieve your goals. Who doesn't want that? Steve Smith, an All-American water polo player and astronaut, puts it this way: "The best role models are the people who have exercised extraordinary discipline to achieve their results. People who refused to be thwarted by failure and who used failures as a spring board to success."

Role models are people you can learn something positive from. They may be one of your peers. They don't necessarily have to be someone you look up to either. Some of life's most valuable lessons can be learned from negative role models, like the guy who got drunk and drove his car into a telephone pole and nearly killed himself. We don't need to make the same kind of mistakes.

> PEOPLE SAY THAT YOU CAN LEARN FROM YOUR OWN MISTAKES. THAT'S TRUE, BUT I'D RATHER LEARN FROM OTHERS' MISTAKES AND LET THEM DEAL WITH THE CONSEQUENCES FOR ME.
> —Linda Toth

Would you agree that people you consider "good" role models are pretty cool? We do. But what actually makes them "cool"? With some insight provided by our buddies at *The Fusion Group*, we will give you a chance to help answer this question.

The *Cool* element

Step 1: Select five people who you think are "cool." They can be famous or just friends from school. (There is no wrong or right answer!)

Step 2: Next to their names, list (briefly) the reasons why you think they are "cool."

Person 1:_____

Reasons:_____

_____

Person 2:_____

Reasons:_____

_____

Person 3:_____

Reasons:_____

_____

Person 4:_____

Reasons:_____

_____

Person 5:_____

Reasons:_____

_____

Step 3: Look over your list, and circle any recurring words. The traits you circle are typically what you define as "cool."

Note: What you discover may surprise you. It sure surprised us. You might find that your answers are very different than what you originally thought was "cool."

In the end, it doesn't matter what kind of car he drives, what brand of clothes she wears, or who so-and-so hangs out with. "Cool" is not something you can do, think about, or buy. Are those people who try to be "cool" actually "cool"? No. Because it's not something you can attempt to do. "Cool" is personal style. It's the way you carry yourself and how you handle the situations you face.

"Cool Stuff"

THE TRUE QUALITY OF A PERSON IS WHAT
THEY DO WHEN NO ONE IS WATCHING.

I WANT IT NOW!

"I don't want to wait! I want it NOW!" Just because a result is not instantly recognizable, it doesn't mean there won't be a result. It's sad, because in reality, it's quite the opposite.

The saying "good things take time" is a useful thought to adopt. Good things do take time. When you have the patience to make the right choices, choices that pay off in the long run, you are on the road to success. Patience is a virtue. It is also the key to achieving what you want out of life.

ONLY THOSE WHO HAVE THE PATIENCE TO
DO SIMPLE THINGS PERFECTLY
EVER ACQUIRE THE SKILL TO DO
DIFFICULT THINGS EASILY.

—Unknown

Most people don't like waiting for results. Our society moves so much faster now than 10 or 20 years ago when it took days or weeks to get a letter in the mail. Today it takes seconds to send a message around the world using e-mail. Our generation is used to instant gratification. We wait only five minutes to get a full meal, 24 hours a day! We have become used to immediate

SNAP SHOT. A picture is worth a 1000 words. Carry a camera with you wherever you go, and capture all those good times.

results. We forget that some things require time. If you want to become better at something, it requires practice, effort, and patience.

PLEASURES OF THE NOW!

People tend to take the easy way out because they can get what we call "pleasures of the now." As humans, we find it natural to seek immediate enjoyment and find a quick fix. Why? Because it's easier than making sacrifices and creating a change in our lives. It's easier to sit down and watch TV instead of studying, practicing sports, or creating worthwhile goals and habits. But will watching another episode of your favorite show propel you down the successful path of life?

Or will you get more from studying and working hard? Hmmm ... Think about how your decisions today will affect your future.

When you decide to change something and work on it, be patient. Expect a delay before you see results. Always remember:

THEY DON'T KNOW

In his book *Think and Grow Rich*, Napoleon Hill says:

> IF THE THING YOU WISH TO DO IS RIGHT,
> AND YOU BELIEVE IN IT, GO AHEAD
> AND DO IT. PUT YOUR DREAMS ACROSS,
> AND NEVER MIND WHAT 'THEY' SAY
> IF YOU MEET WITH TEMPORARY DEFEAT,
> FOR 'THEY,' PERHAPS, DO NOT KNOW THAT
> EVERY FAILURE BRINGS WITH IT THE SEED
> OF AN EQUIVALENT SUCCESS.
>
> — Napoleon Hill

The point is simple: Don't ever let anyone discourage you or rob you of what you need as an individual to be successful.

THE PEOPLE WHO GIVE YOU REASONS
WHY YOU WILL NEVER BE SUCCESSFUL
ARE THE SAME PEOPLE WHO HAVE
NEVER BEEN SUCCESSFUL AND
PROBABLY NEVER WILL BE.

Hint: When you meet people who discourage you, look at them as hecklers yelling from the sidelines of life. They're not even playing the game! They don't know how to play the game! Why listen to them?

THE WRAP

Remove yourself from your comfort zone, and you will discover what you are truly capable of achieving. Don't settle for anything less than success. Be relentless in pursuit of your goals. **Keep this in mind:**

SOME PEOPLE WANT IT TO HAPPEN.
SOME PEOPLE WISH IT WOULD HAPPEN.
SUCCESSFUL PEOPLE MAKE IT HAPPEN.

My "To Do" List:

- ❏ Ditch mediocrity.
- ❏ Constantly step out of my comfort zone.
- ❏ Realize it is okay to fail, as long as I learn.
- ❏ Overcome my fears of failure, and try new things.
- ❏ Hang out with people who will help me
  become a better person.
- ❏ Create an appetite for learning new things.
- ❏ Find my weaknesses, and make them my strengths.
- ❏ Get a role model.
- ❏ My only limits are the ones I give myself.
- ❏ Realize it is possible for anyone to be successful!

"Cool Stuff" I need to take note of:

_____
_____
_____
_____
_____
_____
_____
_____
_____
_____
_____

Attitude

The little thing that makes a BIG difference.

ATTITUDE IS
A CHOICE

IF YOU DON'T LIKE SOMETHING,
CHANGE IT.
IF YOU CAN'T CHANGE IT,
CHANGE YOUR ATTITUDE.
DON'T COMPLAIN.

—Maya Angelou

In most cases, the difference between an ordinary person and a successful person, or between a happy person and a depressed person, is attitude. And attitude is a choice. Think about it ...

Your mindset helps determine the outcome of most situations. This is how it works: Each day is full of different challenges. They can be good, and they can be bad.

It's like poker; you can't determine the cards you are dealt. It's how you play them that matters. You may not be able to control the obstacles that come your way, but more importantly, you can choose how you handle them. The bottom line is:

> "Cool Stuff"
>
> LIFE IS 10% WHAT HAPPENS TO YOU
> AND 90% HOW YOU REACT TO IT.

Now here's a little trick that will allow you to control your attitude in a way that helps you handle life's challenges A LOT better. Just like everyone else, there are certain things (for example, homework) you don't really like to do, but the reason you don't like it lies in the way you look at it. How you perceive things is completely up to you!

When you say, "I have to go to work," "I have to go to practice," or "I have to go to school," you're setting yourself up for a negative experience. Basically you're saying, "I hate this" or "I can't wait until this is over." It's going to be hard to have fun with an attitude like that!

Here's a tip: Be thankful for what you have and what you're able to do! This is not a time to think "Blah, blah, blah." The majority of people in this world do not get the opportunity to go to school, practice, or even work! When you change "I have to" to "I get to," you are changing your mindset—and when you do this, you change your world. Your new attitude kills your old world (negative) and helps you create a new world (positive). You get to have more fun.

Cool Stuff

ATTITUDES ARE LIKE CLOTHES: YOU DECIDE WHAT TO WEAR FOR EACH OCCASION.

Our friend Carlie in Australia was having a hard time staying motivated with work. We talked to her about the "I get to" attitude versus the "I have to" approach, and she immediately picked up on the concept. She started to view her job as a privilege instead of a burden.

After she changed her mindset, she even got a small raise. Carlie believed in the "I get to" concept so much that she shared the idea with Linda and Jessie, twin sisters and very talented up-and-coming singers who were having a hard time staying focused and motivated.

Linda: *My sister and I have been singing since we were three years old. We've been able to travel, record, and experience life in the music industry. We started finding it hard to get up, rehearse, and go to the recording studio every morning.*

Our friend Carlie explained to us the "I get to" versus the "I have to" attitude after she had talked to Kent and Kyle. We never really thought about that concept and decided to try it out. When we applied the idea, we found it much easier to get up, go to recording studios, practice, and maintain the right attitude just by saying "I get to." We had an easier time doing what we in fact actually loved.

"Cool Stuff" ATTITUDE tweaker

Step 1: List the things I previously considered as "have tos." For example: "I have to go to school" or "I have to go practice."

a. I have to_____

b. I have to_____

c. I have to_____

d. I have to_____

e. I have to_____

Step 2: Convert each "I have to" into "I get to."

a. I get to_____

b. I get to_____

c. I get to_____

d. I get to_____

e. I get to_____

BE ENTHUSIASTIC & PASSIONATE

Count on it: People with enthusiasm find life a lot more enjoyable and exciting. How do you get enthusiasm? By deciding you want it!

Create the enthusiasm within yourself by making the effort to get excited about everything you do. And keep doing this until the feeling of enthusiasm becomes a habit. We're not talking about the obnoxious loudmouth at the pep rally. We're talking about genuine and sincere excitement that comes from acknowledging and appreciating how lucky you are to be able to do all the things you do.

According to Richard Carlson, Ph.D., "Enthusiasm is that spark of energy and sense of interest and inspiration that ignites effort, good ideas, intention, creativity, and hard work. *I've found that while it's almost impossible to succeed without it, it's also quite difficult, with enough enthusiasm, to fail.*"

Did you read that last sentence carefully? Thank you, Dr. Carlson!

Enthusiasm is contagious. Could there be a more welcome disease? Everyone loves to be around vibrant people. Bosses love to hire them. People like to help enthusiastic people, so make the decision to become one!

Darrell, a friend of our dad, learned about the importance of being passionate at the company where he works. After years of trial and error, the company found that when hiring new employees, applications, achievements, etc., were not the most important criteria in determining the employees' future success. The most critical criterion was the ability to be passionate.

It didn't matter if an applicant's desire was a hobby outside of work as long as they were excited about it. The company found if a person could be enthusiastic about something, it would also spill into their work. The company grew to become very successful. Perhaps you've heard of it ... a small company called Microsoft.

THE PARALYZING POWER OF YOUR MIND

Your biggest handicaps in life (ours too!) are the negative thoughts you feed your mind. Sounds like the old expression, "Garbage in, garbage out!" In other words:

"Cool Stuff"

IF YOU FEED YOUR MIND NEGATIVE THOUGHTS,
YOU WILL GET NEGATIVE RESULTS.

Or better yet, "Garbage in, garbage stay!" When we constantly think about unconstructive things, that trash doesn't leave our head. Instead, it just piles up and rots our enthusiasm, just as garbage pollutes its surroundings.

Same for you. If you keep piling up your negatives, they'll spread and infect your attitude. With a negative attitude, how likely is it for you to achieve your goals and have fun?

"Cool Stuff"

IF YOU'RE THINKING ABOUT NEGATIVE THINGS,
IT'S HARD TO HAVE POSITIVE EXPERIENCES.

On the other hand, positive thoughts can be extremely powerful. If you believe you will be successful and you work at it, you are more likely to excel. It is that simple. Your mind is the most powerful tool you will ever have! Never underestimate the effect your thoughts can have on your ability to achieve great things.

"I think I can. I think I can. I think I can." Okay, don't laugh. We know you're out of preschool, but do you remember *The Little Engine That Could?* It offers a very important lesson. Have you applied it to your life?

Here is one of our favorite quotes in the entire book. If you understand this, you can instantly expand your potential.

Just as our friend Jennifer was "right" when she kept postponing her driver's license test ... *for four years!*

Now, we know Jennifer well. This young woman has successfully passed all kinds of tests. She is a very talented person. So why did she fail her first driving test?

Jennifer failed because when she thought of driving, she thought of accidents, car troubles, and road rage. Worse, she convinced herself it was impossible for her to pass. No wonder she failed.

Her negative notions made her act nervously and destroyed her confidence. She worried about making a mistake. She didn't pay attention to what she was doing, and she completely missed a stop sign. She fed herself negative thoughts, and those negatives turned into reality.

Enough on negatives! Let's look at the positives. We asked her, "What are the positive aspects of driving? What are your benefits?"

Jennifer named several. She soon associated driving with positive thoughts. In other words, she redirected her focus from negative to positive. Sure enough, her confidence grew. When she took her second test, she paid more attention to her actions (and the traffic signals) instead of just worrying.

Her mindset had shifted. Jennifer could now see the positives. She believed she was going to pass, and she did.

Jennifer's lesson: Sometimes your biggest enemy is yourself ... particularly YOUR MIND.

REALITY CHECK

Jennifer might have received her license even earlier if she had been able to tame the wild and unconstructive thoughts in her brain. When she looked back, she realized the effect her thinking had on her potential to succeed or fail. Her negative thoughts had become so clear and vivid in her head that she believed failing was inevitable!

Jennifer's thoughts had become her reality. The outcome she perceived became true.

Have you ever heard the expression, *"There is no reality, only perception"*? How you see the world is how it actually exists. Every thought and situation you create in your head gives you an impression of each experience you have—good or bad.

Say, for example, your new school year is about to start and you predict that math class is going to be really hard. Guess what? It probably will be. Why? Because your mind doesn't like to be proven wrong. It will focus on everything you find difficult until the class becomes "hard," just like you anticipated.

2K TIP

THANK YOU. When you appreciate what someone did for you, nothing says it better than a handwritten thank-you card. When you're writing your note, make an effort! Spend that extra second to be creative and write something unique. It shows that you genuinely care.

> **"Cool Stuff"**
>
> THE FUTURE WE PERCEIVE FOR OURSELVES WILL OFTEN COME TO PASS.

The situations we build up in our heads will almost certainly come true. Understanding this is extremely important.

So why not perceive a better future? Control your thoughts. Focus on positive things.

Check out this concept:

"Cool Stuff"

YOUR MENTALITY IS YOUR REALITY.

ARE YOU
THE BOSS?

Successful people know how to control their negative thoughts and reject the unconstructive emotions that can potentially hold them back. Your mind is one of the few things you have complete control over. It is something you must learn to manage. You must know when and how to express your feelings.

Sure, every day you'll face challenges that attempt to change your mindset, but **nothing can intrude into your mind without your consent**. Controlling your mind gives you an instant advantage over most people.

"Cool Stuff"

IF YOU CANNOT CONTROL YOUR THOUGHTS,
YOU'LL CONTROL NOTHING ELSE.

Kyle: Here is a great example of how a simple adjustment of your thoughts and attitude can change everything. It was the Saturday night of the winter formal dance for my high school, and I was looking forward to it. It should be fun, right? Well, let me tell you I wasn't thrilled to hear that I had to get up at 6:30 the next morning to go to a water polo tryout. After a long night of dancing, we finally got to bed at 2:30 a.m.

The next morning I was exhausted and extremely unhappy about the day ahead. I said to myself, "Man, I have to drive somewhere I don't want to drive, to be somewhere I don't want to be, to do something I don't want to do." By the time I arrived at the pool, I was in a depressed state as I listened to the whistles screaming and the coaches droning on and on.

I shook Jeff, who was fighting to stay awake, and said, "We better change our attitudes and try to have a little fun today, or else this is going to be hell." So we did.

2K TIP

DRINK UP. Feelin' tired? The #1 cause of daytime fatigue is dehydration. Keep that water bottle full and within reach. It's good for you, and it gives you energy. What do you have to lose besides ill health and drowsiness?

We were both surprised to notice how we immediately started having a great time. The day actually turned out to be a lot of fun. The simple decision to look for the best not only changed our outlook but our performance as well.

You must be able to control what will affect you and what won't. If you let the world walk all over you and give it the power to choose your attitude for you, your mindset will be negative.

Now, just how can you become the boss of your own life and call all the shots? *Here are the three main steps to taking control:*

1 Search. Let's get something straight: Managing your mind is simply overpowering your negative emotions so you can feel good

and in control. The first step in managing your mind is searching for the things that can instantly uplift your soul.

Think back to a time when you felt the world had turned its back on you … when your boyfriend or girlfriend dumped you, or you failed that big test. At those moments, did you notice all the good things that were happening around you at the same time? Was the sun shining? Were you healthy? Did you have friends or family that cared about you?

Most people can't remember, because, as we said earlier, it's hard to notice good things when you're focusing on feeling bad. But by making an effort to search for and focus on all those positive things, you can shift your mindset to a more positive outlook.

2 *Ask yourself.* "What am I happy about right now?" When you ask yourself this simple question, you empower yourself. Or if you are feeling really down, you might rephrase your question slightly: "What could I be happy about?" That's what it's all about—finding what makes you feel good!

The state of mind you're in determines how you see the world around you. When you're sad, isn't everything a drag? When you're happy and excited, don't things seem to be more fun and interesting? The trick is getting out of the sad, tired, angry, and upset states and freeing your positive emotions, such as happiness, creativeness, passion, and enthusiasm. It all starts by discovering the things you can be grateful for at any given moment.

Kent: Kyle and I experience instant satisfaction simply by reminding ourselves of the small things we often take for granted. We're happy knowing that we have the opportunity to breathe, the fact we were born in a free country, and we have a roof over our head. There are a gazillion things that anyone can feel good about at any moment in time. It's just a matter of bringing them to mind and making them your focus of attention.

3 **Remember.** Finding all these uplifting things is extremely important. However, they don't do much good if you can't remember or recall them when you need them. Learn how to remember them by filling out the Smile Builder on the next page. Memorize your discoveries!

By mastering these concepts, you will eliminate a ton of stress and frustration. Make sure you fight to keep a positive perspective, because a negative outlook is just a giant speed bump in the road to success.

> ABILITY IS WHAT YOU'RE
> CAPABLE OF DOING.
> MOTIVATION DETERMINES
> WHAT YOU DO.
> ATTITUDE DETERMINES
> HOW WELL YOU DO IT.
> —Lou Holtz

"Cool Stuff" SMILE builder

Step 1: List five things you are grateful for ... anything that makes you feel good when you think about them.

a. _____

b. _____

c. _____

d. _____

e. _____

Step 2: Remember the things you wrote down. Refer back to this sheet if you have to, but make sure you can recall these things when you feel down and need to smile again.

HOW DO YOU SEE IT?

The people who excel in life are those who look at each difficulty as an opportunity to learn something new. Ever get irritated over a roadblock and not being able to take your usual route? Instead, you can choose to view this as an opportunity to discover a new restaurant or store or park that you would have otherwise missed.

On a bigger scale, some remarkable people have overcome great challenges like serious health issues, poverty, drug addiction, growing up without parents, and so on. In fact, some people believe that those very challenges can be attributed to their success.

Take Lance Armstrong, for example. How could he be "thankful" he got cancer? His medications and treatments must have clouded his judgment! Only after thinking about it did we understand what he meant. The cancer caused Lance to search for more inner strength and personal faith. His ill health challenged him to grow stronger mentally and develop the confidence necessary to win the next Tour de France.

We firmly believe that:

"Cool Stuff"

CIRCUMSTANCES CAN SHAPE PEOPLE, BUT MORE IMPORTANTLY THEY REVEAL WHO THEY REALLY ARE.

"Once upon a time . . ."

No, wait ... that sounds corny. Let's start again. "It was a dark and stormy night . . . " No, that's even worse! Hmmm . . . Okay, here we go:

Twin brothers grew up in the same house with alcoholic parents. When they grew up, one brother became an alcoholic and the other a successful, healthy person. When the alcoholic brother was asked what happened to him, he replied, "What do you expect? I grew up with alcoholic parents." The successful brother was asked the same question and he replied, "What do you expect? I grew up with alcoholic parents. I saw that it wasn't the lifestyle I wanted."

negative   positive   optimistic

In the end, what makes the biggest difference is the way you look at challenges and the attitude you decide to use when you deal with them. How do you see things? Is the glass half empty or half full?

Or is the glass twice as big as it should be?

> I HAVE LEARNED THAT SUCCESS IS TO BE MEASURED NOT SO MUCH BY THE POSITION ONE HAS REACHED IN LIFE AS BY THE OBSTACLES WHICH ONE HAS OVERCOME WHILE TRYING TO SUCCEED.
>
> —Booker T. Washington

AJ, one of our friends, learned the true meaning of Booker T. Washington's words. AJ suffered a horrific accident and lost his legs. Amazingly, he refused to let the situation hold him back from accomplishing his dreams and living a happy life.

Let AJ tell you his story:

AJ: *As soon as I entered my early teens, I got in some trouble with the law and ended up doing some jail time. Let's just say I wasn't the most obedient kid and didn't have a very good outlook on life. I learned my lesson the hard way.*

At age seventeen, I lost my legs in a motorcycle accident and had a very important choice to make: feel sorry for myself and be miserable for the rest of my life or be glad I was still alive. Fortunately, I chose to have a positive attitude and focused on all the things I could be grateful for.

The accident gave me a completely new outlook. I learned how important it was to look for the good in all situations, because life is just too short and valuable to mourn and focus on how things could be better. It really put my problems into perspective and made me realize everything can always be worse, so be thankful for what you've been dealt.

Only nine months after his accident, AJ placed third in a triathlon. He travels around the USA to compete in triathlons and marathons where he consistently achieves first place. AJ also prequalified for six Para Olympic events in swimming and continues to succeed in other areas of his life.

Whenever we see AJ, he is smiling. He is a perfect example of how the right attitude can drastically change your life. The beauty of this is that you don't need something horrific to happen in order to realize this. Choose to have the right attitude today!

THE WRAP

When you decide to have a positive outlook, new possibilities will open up for you. You will be capable of doing things you never thought possible. Attitude is the little thing that makes a BIG difference. With the right mindset, you'll find you can achieve more of your goals, excel in your job or school, have better friendships, and lead a more enjoyable life. Sound good? It is! Sound too good? Then you need to adjust your attitude.

My "To Do" List:

❑ Say "I get to" instead of "I have to."

❑ Choose to be enthusiastic and passionate about what I do.

❑ Feed my mind positive thoughts so I can have positive experiences.

❑ If I think I can or think I can't, I'm right.

❑ Look at life's challenges with a positive and open-minded approach ... view them as opportunities to learn something new.

❑ Control my thoughts so I can control my life.

❑ Realize I have control over the outcome of my life!

Goals & Habits
03

You create your habits
... and your habits
create you.

YOU CREATE YOUR HABITS

"**Y**ou create your habits ..." That's the good news.

"**... And your habits create you.**" That could be good or bad. It depends on you.

You decide what habits to create. The key point here is that most people form habits, both good and bad, without even realizing it. Forming good habits, of course, will help you. And forming bad habits will make you your own worst enemy.

We're guessing you want the good habits, right? Well, if you do, read on to find out how to make your goals and habits work for you.

> "Cool Stuff"
>
> OUR THOUGHTS DETERMINE OUR ACTIONS.
> OUR ACTIONS DETERMINE OUR HABITS.
> OUR HABITS DETERMINE OUR CHARACTER.
> AND OUR CHARACTER DETERMINES
> OUR DESTINY.

Kyle: *I know two guys who know the importance of goal-setting. They studied, read, wrote, and spoke about the value of goals and goal-setting but had not really put it all into practice.*

After realizing they should take their own advice, they took the time to write down their goals. Once they did, they were extremely surprised. It became easier for them to work through difficult situations, stay focused, and get things done because they knew what they wanted and how to get it.

We know these people really well. These "people" are my brother and me.

ARE GOALS REALLY
THAT IMPORTANT?

Much of your future depends on two things: the goals you choose and the habits you create. Goals give you a target to shoot for. For example, in sports, the goal is where players score; without a goal, there is nowhere to score ... no way to play the game.

Life is a game too – the most important one you'll ever play! Don't you want to win?

Without goals, you're a bystander or a spectator, watching your own life. How can you possibly "win"? You could have the greatest attitude, the strongest passion, and all the enthusiasm in the world, but if you don't direct your energy, all that effort is wasted.

The Cheshire Cat said it best:

IF YOU DON'T KNOW WHERE YOU WANT TO GO, ANY ROAD WILL TAKE YOU THERE.

Don't just drift through life like a jellyfish. Be a wave with direction and power. Otherwise you'll never be satisfied with where you are and where you are going. Nothing rewarding happens by chance. If you wait for someone to motivate you, you will be waiting a long, long time ... because it won't happen!

YOU DECIDE

Here's the bottom line: No one is going to make you do anything. They can try, but they cannot force you to create worthwhile habits. Going through life without positive goals and habits is like trying to push a piece of cooked spaghetti.

You have no control over its direction. Do you really want that? Decide to make good habits on your own (and *not* just to keep your parents off your back!).

Why do people like your parents keep nagging at you to "do this," "do that," and "do it this way" over and over again? No, not to annoy you, but because they want to help you make your life easier.

There's nothing in it for them other than the satisfaction of passing useful information to you that they have learned along the way.

> **"Cool Stuff"**
>
> THIS WORLD REWARDS ACTION.
> IT IS ALWAYS LOOKING FOR THE PEOPLE
> WHO CAN MAKE DECISIONS ON THEIR
> OWN AND GET THINGS DONE!

Instead, give yourself the opportunity to enjoy the process. Decide to make your own goals and to create good habits. Be independent and in control of your life.

THE FIRST TIME IS ALWAYS THE HARDEST

Of course, you already knew this from experience. It's true: The first time is the hardest. Creating habits is not easy. Habits require a lot of repetition and discipline, but once you get past the "first time" and get rolling, you are on your way.

Even though the first time may be the most difficult, it's also the easiest time to make or break a habit. Remember, the best way to break a bad habit is not to start it in the first place. Create habits that you will benefit from, like being organized, being punctual, and setting goals.

Ever notice how difficult it is to go back to school and start studying each night after a long summer break? What happened to the rhythm you had during the last school year? Gone! The same goes for sports. Training can be hard work at the beginning; sometimes the hardest part is deciding to show up. After the first few times, it becomes easier. Remember this whenever you find it hard to follow through with something.

GOALS CREATE
OPPORTUNITIES!

We had a problem. We were planning a cross-country trip, and we wanted dirt-jumping (BMX) bikes before we left. The problem? We could not afford them.

When you work toward something, your subconscious mind searches for ways to make it possible and shows you new opportunities. How could we earn money quickly for the bikes? Getting bikes before our trip became our new goal.

While we were brainstorming in my dad's office, it hit us. As we were looking out the windows, we realized how dirty they were. "Dad, will you pay us to wash these windows?" Pause ... "Thanks, Dad!"

Next: Quick stop at Home Depot. Squeegees, sponges, rags, cleaner, buckets. Add some hard work, and soon the windows were finished. We were holding our paychecks! Wait ... it gets better!

Now that we had all this window-washing equipment, it would be a shame to waste our capital investment. Surely other office buildings around Silicon Valley had dirty windows. Would they hire Mario & Squeegee Bros. (our new company name)?

Yeah, we earned enough for the bikes. Best of all, we were making three times as much as we would have earned flipping burgers or working as lifeguards.

Because we had a goal (getting bikes for our trip), we saw an opportunity to create our own business, make money, and have fun at the same time.

EVERYBODY, SOMEBODY, ANYBODY, AND NOBODY

This is a story of four people—Everybody, Somebody, Anybody, and Nobody. One day Everybody was asked to do an important job. Everybody was sure Somebody would do it. Everybody knew, after all, that Anybody could have done it. But in fact, Nobody did it. Well, Somebody got angry about that, because after all, it was Everybody's job.

In truth, Nobody realized Everybody wouldn't do it. It ended up that Everybody blamed Somebody, because Nobody did what Anybody could have done.

Successful people rely on habits and goals. They set a goal for exactly what they want to achieve and create habits that make it happen. They know that without both habits and goals, they will go nowhere, get nothing done, and become frustrated.

"Cool Stuff"

SUCCESSFUL PEOPLE ARE SUCCESSFUL BECAUSE THEY ARE WILLING TO MAKE HABITS OUT OF THE THINGS UNSUCCESSFUL PEOPLE ARE UNWILLING TO DO.

DEAL WITH IT!

Why *don't* people achieve their goals?

1 Dwelling on the Past. The main reason is that they dwell on the past and collect the scars of failure. If you screw up, you can't go back. When history is made, no amount of worrying can change it, so put failures behind you, learn from them, and move on.

2 Blame Others. It's all too easy to blame others. Don't! You're better off saying nothing. If you really think about it, who likes to hear excuses? No one. Excuses only accomplish one thing: They make you look bad. Do complainers get any sympathy? No!

3 Ignore 'Em! Ignoring your problems doesn't make them go away. Instead, ignoring them just gives them a chance to grow into larger challenges. Life definitely does not reward those who act like ostriches and stick their head in the ground hoping their problems just disappear.

Avoiding your difficulties may work in the short run, but it always catches up with you. Matters will only become worse for you and for everyone else.

"Cool Stuff"

NEGATIVITY DESTROYS YOUR ABILITY TO ACHIEVE POSITIVE THINGS.

Sarah: *At the beginning of last year, I set a goal to get straight A's. However, I got off to a bad start and failed my first important English and physics tests. I was fuming. I couldn't believe it. Instead of putting it behind me and focusing on the next tests, I kept wondering why, why, why?*

Before long, I was extremely frustrated and found myself trying to justify my problem by blaming other people. I no longer enjoyed going to class, and my goal of getting straight A's began to fade away.

Since I didn't deal with my problem immediately, I didn't do very well on my next tests either. Then, out of the blue, my teacher approached me and said, "Sarah, what's going on? You're better than this." I sure got a reality check. My teacher helped me realize that I had been focusing on the problem rather than the solution. While I was doing this, my problem had been growing unknowingly.

2K TIP

DELIVERY SERVICE. Pick up the newspaper on the way to the front door—especially at your friend's house. Parents will love it, and it shows you're not living in la-la-land oblivious to your surroundings.

I recognized that my negative attitude was the only thing keeping me from achieving my goal. With some effort, I changed my outlook, got tutoring, worked with my teachers, and did all the extra credit I could. I didn't get straight A's, but I did learn a really important lesson that will help me reach my next goals faster. I discovered the significance of dealing with my troubles as soon as possible—before they get out of control. Like Kent and Kyle say, acting negatively robs us of our opportunities to achieve positive things.

THE BAD ONES

Avoiding bad habits is just as important as creating good ones. Bad habits often cancel out good ones. It's silly to develop the habit of brushing your teeth before bed if you have a bad habit of secret snacking during the night!

The first step in avoiding a bad habit is to become aware of it. Of course, everybody has some bad habits; nobody is perfect.

When you look for these weaknesses, you're allowing yourself to improve. If you deny your weaknesses or don't recognize them (like our friend), you kill your chance to become the person you can be.

"I was only trying to help."

Observe your actions—or even better, ask successful individuals you respect for their opinions. Most of us don't like to ask others about our weaknesses because we're afraid of the answers. Sure, it is uncomfortable, but it's one of the quickest ways to produce results. What others tell you might really help you reach your goals faster.

Caution 1: This does not work if you are defensive. Just listen. Be open to change.

Caution 2: Don't waste time telling others about their bad habits. Yes, you may think you're doing them a favor, but if they haven't asked you for your opinion, don't share it. They'll think you're being critical—not to mention being a jerk.

DREAM
DREAM

> *"Cool Stuff"*
>
> IF YOU WANT A DREAM TO COME TRUE,
> YOU FIRST MUST HAVE A DREAM.

Kyle: *Kent and I have our own vision boards to help us stay focused. On Kent's board are pictures and statements of what he wants out of life. My board has mine. Every time we become distracted or frustrated when things don't go as well as we want, we look at our vision board. It motivates us to keep going.*

"Cool Stuff" MOTIVATOR Inflator

How big are your dreams? How bad do you want them?

Step 1: Get a big piece of cardboard.

Step 2: Collect pictures, statements, etc., that inspire you. Be creative.

Step 3: Slap your findings onto the board. Frame it if you want.

Step 4: Put your masterpiece on the wall. Find out what a vision board can do for you. It sure helped us!

Kent: *My dad walked into my room when I was making my vision board. I had a piece of cardboard four feet by two feet with pictures of houses on the beach, nice cars, tropical beaches, good waves, and famous people. He said, "You know, Kent, if you had a board half that size, you'd be done by now." I replied, "I know, but I have big dreams."*

Dreams lead to goals, and goals to happiness. They create desire—the fire within you to keep you working when you don't want to. It is like a reward for your effort and work. Sorry, but you don't find a dream by sleeping. You have to picture what you want out of life.

A dream is a vision. Where do you see yourself in ten years? Do you have your own house? A Ferrari? Or maybe something less elaborate and more practical like a nice apartment and a good reliable car? Fine, but little will come your way without identifying your dream and setting a goal to get there.

Most people aren't aware that we all have a dream inside waiting to be found. It's not really a matter of if you have a dream. It is there! The question should be, "What is your dream?"

Well, what are *your* dreams? Search for your dreams, and work towards reaching them.

> *"Cool Stuff"*
>
> YOUR DREAMS AND YOUR EFFORTS TO REACH THEM WILL DETERMINE YOUR SUCCESS IN LIFE. THIS IS NOT SOMETHING THAT HAPPENS BY LUCK OR FATE.

If your dreams seem almost impossible to reach, DON'T be discouraged! It's okay. Be imaginative and creative. When you dream, you're looking at the "big picture" of your life. It is natural to feel intimidated by your visions. That's why we break dreams down into smaller steps ... called goals. As you have probably heard by now, every journey begins with a single step. Each goal you reach moves you forward, one step closer to your dream.

THE EASY WAY OUT

> "Cool Stuff"
>
> IT'S EASIER TO WORK AROUND GOALS THAN TO WORK AROUND PROBLEMS.

Many people never reach their goals because things get too hard. In other words, "the going gets tough." Well, duhhh ... of course you'll face hard times! Most people want to be successful, yet they continue to follow their same old ways.

2K TIP

WORK FAST ... work efficiently. Procrastination is a silent killer. People complain that they don't have enough time, but in a lot of cases, they're just really good at l-e-n-g-t-h-e-n-i-n-g quick and easy tasks. If there is work to be done, don't daydream about it. Get into it, get it done, and get the weight off your shoulders. "Do it. Do it. Do it."
– Starsky & Hutch

If you think your journey is going to be hard, you're right. It almost certainly will be. You will have to change your habits so you can reach your goals. Use the well-known formula for success: work hard, focus, be enthusiastic, and never give up. As Benjamin Franklin once said, most people work hard only to give up just before success.

BLUEPRINTS

The greatest thing about goals is that they give you the opportunity to create now the life you want in the near future. In other words, goals give you the opportunity to design the blueprints of your own life in advance. How valuable is that?! You can't build a house without plans, so you can't expect to build your life without them either.

Something happens when you write down your goals. It's unexplainable ... or at least beyond our understanding. Tony Robbins, author and authority on peak performance, tells a great story that describes what we mean:

In 1953, there was a fascinating study done at Yale University. Just before the graduating class left school, they were interviewed and asked a bunch of questions, but the one that really jumped out was, "How many of you have a clear, specific set of goals, with a written plan for their achievement?"

The answer was shocking! Less than 3% had written goals with a set plan. Twenty years later, in 1973, the graduates from the class of '53 were interviewed once again. They were asked what their lives were like now that they had been out of school for quite a while.

The findings were very interesting. The 3% that had written goals and had a clear plan to reach them appeared to be happier about their direction, their accomplishments, and their life in general.

Even more surprising was the fact that the 3% of people who had written goals were worth more financially than the other 97% ... combined!

Amazing! This is the effect that goal-setting can have on your life.

We have seen a huge improvement in our lives since we've set our own goals. It's practically transformed us! We've learned that you can know all the self-improvement methods and all the tricks-of-the-trade, but if you don't have the clear purpose or direction that goals give you, you won't reach full potential.

"Cool Stuff"

GOALS ARE NOTHING BUT DREAMS WITH DEADLINES.

Take the first step right now, and design your own blueprints. Come on ... it's easy. Remember, this is your chance to create in advance the future you want.

To get the most out of this exercise, your goals should:

>> Be realistic, but challenging too.
>> Inspire and motivate you to complete them.
>> Have a specific deadline.

Note: Fill out the following ~~work~~playsheets. Read them often to remind yourself of your future direction. You wouldn't drive somewhere you've never been without a map, right? Well, your future is undiscovered too, so these goals are maps, life maps. Don't waste your life drifting.

Fill these out, get your bearings, head toward your destination, and give yourself the chance to reach your full potential!

Goal #1

1. My Goal: _____

_____

_____

2. I will reach this goal by _____ (specific date).

3. What will I get by reaching this goal? How will my life become better? (Think hard, because this will help inspire and motivate you to follow through. If you complete this goal, what are the things you will be excited about?)

a._____

_____

b._____

_____

c._____

_____

4. What will I miss out on if I don't follow through and make a full commitment to my goal? What are the costs of giving up?

a._____

_____

b._____

_____

c._____

_____

5. What steps should I take or what habits should I create to achieve my goal faster and easier?

a._____

_____

b._____

_____

6. What is ONE action I can take today that will bring me closer to achieving my goal?

_____

_____

Goal #2

1. My Goal: _____

_____

_____

2. I will reach this goal by _____(specific date).

3. What will I get by reaching this goal? How will my life become better? (Think hard, because this will help inspire and motivate you to follow through. If you complete this goal, what are the things you will be excited about?)

a._____

_____

b._____

_____

c._____

_____

4. What will I miss out on if I don't follow through and make a full commitment to my goal? What are the costs of giving up?

a._____

_____

b._____

_____

c._____

_____

5. What steps should I take or what habits should I create to achieve my goal faster and easier?

a._____

_____

b._____

_____

6. What is ONE action I can take today that will bring me closer to achieving my goal?

_____

_____

Goal #3

1. My Goal: _____

_____

_____

2. I will reach this goal by _____(specific date).

3. What will I get by reaching this goal? How will my life become better? (Think hard, because this will help inspire and motivate you to follow through. If you complete this goal, what are the things you will be excited about?)

a._____

_____

b._____

_____

c._____

_____

4. What will I miss out on if I don't follow through and make a full commitment to my goal? What are the costs of giving up?

a._____

_____

b._____

_____

c._____

_____

5. What steps should I take or what habits should I create to achieve my goal faster and easier?

a._____

_____

b._____

_____

6. What is ONE action I can take today that will bring me closer to achieving my goal?

_____

_____

THE WRAP

Decisions, goals, and habits are closely related. You can't follow through with *goals* and create or change *habits* unless you *decide* to. You need all three things to get what you want out of life. Create good habits and set goals to build a promising future for yourself.

> "Cool Stuff"
>
> THE DIFFERENCE BETWEEN WINNERS AND LOSERS IS THEIR HABITS, GOALS, AND EFFORTS TO REACH THEM.

My "To Do" List:

❏ Realize the huge effect goals and habits have on my life.

❏ Decide to make good goals and habits on my own.

❏ Take action on my own life, because the world does not owe me anything!

❏ Realize that the first few attempts to make a habit or set a goal will be the hardest, so I won't become discouraged.

❏ Discover and change what I don't like about myself, because if I don't, my life will never improve.

❏ Avoid being Everybody, Somebody, Anybody, or Nobody. Get things done!

❏ Make habits of the things unsuccessful people are unwilling to do.

❏ Let go of the past and grab hold of the present.

❏ Create a vision board to help me stay focused.

❏ Design the blueprints for my life by filling out the three goal playsheets!

"Cool Stuff" I need to take note of:

_____

_____

_____

_____

_____

_____

_____

Feelin' the Pressure?

04

C'mon, read this.
We dare you!

EVERYBODY'S DOING IT

Come on, man! Everybody's doing it. If you don't read this chapter, you're a loser!

Every time we changed schools, moved to a different city, or experienced a new culture, we received a welcoming gift: peer pressure. It's kind of like the Christmas gift from Grandma. You know ... the unique, hand-knitted, one-of-a-kind sweater with a "COOL" reindeer on the front. Yeah, right! Thanks a lot!

Peer pressure is something nobody wants but everybody gets. Just about every time it is mentioned, people roll their eyes and say, "Ha—that doesn't affect me!" But it does. We all know it exists, and believe it or not, everyone is affected by it. Just look at the way you dress, the group you hang out with, the music you listen to, even what you eat. Don't believe it? Take a second to imagine what your life would be like if others didn't influence you at all ... heck, you'd probably throw on that unsightly reindeer sweater!

If you think peer pressure is limited to school and to your teenage years, you're wrong! It will be with you your entire life; it is part of the real world. How you deal with it now will determine how you deal with it for the rest of your life. That's a long time to carry around worthless trash, so why not get rid of it now?

Watch out, though … peer pressure isn't always visible. People aren't really going to say, "C'mon, you loser, try this, or I won't be your friend." They save that stuff for Hollywood and pamphlets written by out-of-touch university professors. No. Real peer pressure comes in different forms. It can be sly, so you'd better know how to recognize it.

Kent: *Ah, science class! Always out of the ordinary. On a typical day, some students sprayed pools of deodorant on their desks and then lit them, competing for the biggest flame. Meanwhile, if the teacher was out of the room, students in the back were busy using the Bunsen burners to light up their joints. Utter chaos!*

I'll never forget my days at this high school I attended. There was always some drug deal going on. The classroom had more marijuana than pens, pencils, and paper. It seemed to be a dietary supplement for these guys. But that wasn't the craziest thing I noticed.

I noticed pressure to do drugs and join in on their crazy games, but the pressure wasn't coming directly from my classmates. They never said, "Come on, everybody's doing it!" They never said, "If you don't do this, you're a loser."

No, the "pressure" was actually coming from me! I felt a strong but unconscious need to become part of the group, to fit in. Luckily I recognized it before I fell into the trap. I learned a valuable lesson:

"Cool Stuff"

PEER PRESSURE IS CUNNING.

It may not be in your face and easy to identify. It can come from within you—so be prepared.

JUST BEAT IT!

Changing schools often meant that we were exposed to more forms of peer pressure than normal. Gradually, we discovered what worked and what didn't. So what is the best way to defeat peer pressure? Build (and then rely on) your own self-confidence.

You might be saying, "I've already heard that!" We're pretty sure you have. But have you acted on it? Does your everyday personality shout confidence to others? Most of us think so. However, the way we perceive ourselves is often different from the way other people perceive us.

It's like watching a video of yourself. Sometimes the person on screen simply does not look like ME. You might think you walk different, sound different, and look different than you thought. Do you see what we mean? You need to pay extra attention to the way you carry yourself. Because after all, **you determine how others treat you!** In order to get treated the way you want to be, you need to do two things:

1 Give others the respect you'd like to have from them.

2 Be happy and comfortable with who you are—your values, beliefs, and actions.

PEOPLE THINK IT'S THEIR SURROUNDINGS THAT MAKE THEM FEEL UNEASY. HOWEVER, IF YOU FEEL COMFORTABLE WITH WHO YOU ARE, YOU'LL FEEL COMFORTABLE WITH WHERE YOU ARE.

—Linda Toth

Your level of confidence determines your level of protection. How do you get it? It originates from your personal belief system. It all goes back to what you believe to be true about yourself. That's why it is so important to believe in what you do and to build that self-esteem.

"Cool Stuff"

WE FOUND THAT GETTING CONFIDENCE IS MORE OF A DECISION THAN A DISCOVERY.

Your confidence shows in many ways. You'll need strong body language, eye contact, and a firm tone of voice to come out on top and in control. Why? Because these are the things that will affect the way other people treat you.

So . . . how do you want to be treated?

If you come across as insecure, others will notice it right away. People will try to pressure you if they think you will give in. It's a bummer, but it's true. You're far less likely to be a victim of peer pressure if you're confident about yourself, your beliefs, and your values. Offer a firm handshake, look people in the eye, and stand up for your values. After all, it *is* your life.

BACK 'EM UP!

W hen you are being pressured, don't you wish someone would step in to bail you out? Well, it works the same way in reverse. Stand up for others—especially when you see them in uncomfortable situations. Put yourself in their shoes, and think about how you would feel.

Back them up. No one likes to be pressured. If you agree, don't be afraid to jump in and rescue them. A team of two is a lot more effective than an individual.

"Cool Stuff"

YOU'RE ACTUALLY CONTRIBUTING TO
PEER PRESSURE BY IGNORING IT
WHEN YOU CAN HELP.

PEACE OF MIND

Time for some advice! You can't be right all the time. Sometimes you'll need to take advice. (Wait ... there's more.) As a result, it's important to ask people you trust. Who you approach is purely up to you, so choose wisely.

Our experience has shown that most junior high or middle school students turn to their parents for advice about peer pressure; older students usually go to friends. That's fine, as long as your friend has your best interests at heart. But be careful! **A friend will often give you the answer they think you want to hear—or the answer that makes them look cool.** Speak to people or friends you think will have honest advice, not just answers you want to hear.

And let's be fair to parents. Parents don't stop giving good advice just because they're older. In fact, the older they get, the more experience and knowledge they have to offer. Think about it: Are you smarter and wiser today than you were five years ago? So are your parents—and grandparents. Tap into that lifetime of knowledge and experience!

Perhaps you're thinking, "What do I do if people ask me for advice?"

Well, first make sure they really want to hear your advice. Then, give it to them *honestly*, but tell them it's only your opinion and you're not a psychiatrist with a degree ... unless, of course, you really are.

Always seek to help, *not* **to please.** If you give the advice you think they want to hear, you're buckling to peer pressure yourself.

TRUST YOUR INSTINCTS

Most of the time when you ask for advice, you already know the right answer; you just wish the answer was different. This is your gut instinct yelling at you, and it's an important tool to use in beating negative peer pressure. In a situation where you feel something's wrong, you're probably right.

All we can say is stick up for what you believe is right. It's up to you. Learn to trust your instincts, and let them influence you more than somebody else.

IF YOU DON'T STAND FOR SOMETHING,
YOU'LL FALL FOR ANYTHING.

ARM YOURSELF

O ne of the best ways to conquer peer pressure is to think ahead. Try to avoid situations that might put you in an awkward position. Is it likely that a certain situation will make you question your values or go against your will? If you believe it might, avoid it.

Again, listen to your conscience, and pay attention to what you feel, not what you want to hear. Make the right choice from the start, so one bad decision doesn't lead to another.

PREPARATION IS KEY

Y es, there surely will be times when you don't have a choice and you find yourself in an uncomfortable situation. The best solution is to be prepared before you get into it. For example, at some point in your life, you will probably face the issue of drugs. How are you going to handle the situation? Are you going to do what you believe is right, or are you going to let other people influence you?

Ya want some?

Here's the worst part: **The *right* decision probably won't be an easy one**. Be prepared, think ahead, and have answers ready for questions and situations you predict might challenge your beliefs. You may not be able to come up with everything, but you could sure cover a lot. Having some answers is better than no answers.

Tip: Ask your friends, parents, relatives, or teachers about some of the tough situations they had to face. What did they do? Did it work? What should they have done differently? There's an old adage that says:

> THE SMART MAN LEARNS FROM HIS MISTAKES; THE WISE MAN LEARNS FROM OTHERS' MISTAKES.

The answers you come up with will reflect what you truly believe because no one will have the chance to influence your thoughts. By thinking ahead, you will have more time to look at the consequences of your choices, and then you'll feel more comfortable with the decision you make.

YOUR FELLOWSHIP

Sometimes you'll find yourself making decisions you never would have made in the past.

Our ideals change as we get older, but usually these changes will unknowingly come from the people we associate with. We've already mentioned how the people we spend time with will influence our personality, beliefs, and values.

Hang out with people who share your interests; avoid those that don't respect your values. That doesn't mean you should completely ignore the people who don't think exactly like you! It is very important to try to get along with everybody, but don't spend too much time with people who might drag you down.

KNOW WHO YOU ARE

W e all know people who have made the wrong choice in order to "fit in." It's not pretty. We have a friend who changes depending on the group he is with. With one group he's the "cool/sly" kind of guy, and with another, he's a "comedian" or sometimes a "tough guy." He sometimes appears confident, but his actions betray him. When we see him try to fit into so many groups, it's obvious he's pretty insecure. Don't change yourself in an effort to "belong." Don't even think about it!

> **"Cool Stuff"**
>
> TRYING TO PLEASE EVERYONE
> IS THE KEY TO FAILURE.

As victims of peer pressure, we had to make a choice ... the same choice everyone must make at some point in their lives: to try and instantly impress people, or be ourselves and attract friends who like us because of who we were.

Sounds corny, but hey, **if you want *real* friends, you have to be your *real* self.**

THE WRAP

P eer pressure all comes down to making the right decisions when you feel something's wrong. Make sure the decisions you make are yours and not someone else's. If anyone ever says to you, "everybody's doing it," ask yourself:

DO I WANT TO BE EVERYBODY OR DO I WANT TO BE SOMEBODY?

everyone   someone

My "To Do" List:

❏ Realize that peer pressure has different forms. It can come from within me and still involve my peers.

❏ Become immune to peer pressure by building my self-confidence.

❏ How I decide to use my body language, eye contact, and tone of voice will determine how others treat me.

❏ Bail other people out of uncomfortable situations.

❏ Approach people who will give the right and honest advice, not just what they think I want to hear.

❏ When I give advice, I'll always seek to help, not please.

❏ Trust and listen to my instincts because if I feel something's wrong, I'm probably right.

❏ Avoid potentially awkward situations.

❏ Be prepared for situations I'll probably face.

❏ Be comfortable and confident with who I am.

Make Yourself the
#1 Applicant

Get what you want
with the job
you want!

A JOB MEANS
INDEPENDENCE

Sooner or later, most of us will need to find a job. Bills need to be paid, cars need to be purchased, spending money needs to be found. Let's face it, a job means independence—unless you prefer living at home at age 25 and being told to "eat your veggies" and "be home by 11 o'clock!"

The good news is that working doesn't have to be a drag. What do you like? If you like surfing, apply for a job at a surf shop. Like bikes? Get a job at a bike shop. Like food? How about a restaurant?

> **"Cool Stuff"**
>
> IF YOU FIND A JOB YOU LIKE,
> YOU'LL NEVER WORK A DAY IN YOUR LIFE.

Even for experienced people, the thought of applying for a

job can be scary. Who enjoys filling out applications in stuffy offices or greasy food outlets, being grilled by adults, and then maybe hearing you didn't get the position? But like anything else in life, the more prepared you are, the greater your chance of success.

We decided to improve our odds of getting a job by interviewing managers and business owners to find out what they look for in their employees. Some of the things they told us were obvious, but others were quite surprising. Believe it or not, we learned some really interesting stuff.

So here's the inside story from employers plus some secret steps to getting the job you want.

THE IMPORTANCE OF ATTITUDE AND "WANTING" A JOB

Usually the hardest part of getting a job is deciding to get one. (Caution: Attitude speech ahead!) The right attitude truly helps. This is when you decide whether your work is going to be fun or just a "job."

I want a job!

Get excited about working and earning money! It's a cool feeling when you get a paycheck you earned. This is what being an independent person is all about. So set your personal expectations high, be eager to work, want to get a job, and you will be happy with your results.

Now that you have decided you WANT a job, where do you start? Well, what are you interested in? If you don't like fried food and talking to people, a fast-food joint is probably not your first choice.

Ready to start? First, make a list of the people you know. Who can hook you up with a job? The fancy word for this is *networking*. It's much easier to get a job through networking, because getting in the door is often the hardest part. When you're looking for a job, tell your friends, family, and neighbors. Use your connections. People who know you are more likely to help you.

Here's how you network. Let's say you know someone in a business or industry you would like to work in. If you *ask that person directly* for a job, you're putting him or her in an awkward position. Better: Ask him or her for advice on getting into their industry.

For example, let's say "Mrs. Vogue" is in the fashion business. Politely ask her, "What's the best way to go about getting a job in the fashion industry?" "Where can I apply?" "Whom should I speak with?" "What should I do?" People in business are usually willing to share their experience and offer advice, so be patient and polite.

Tip 1: Whenever someone does help you, send a thank-you letter! You will make a good impression, and you will be remembered. If they are impressed with you, they just might say, "Why don't you come work for me?"

Tip 2: Be careful who you ask! You may not want to approach the old lady two doors down who saw you tie cans to her cat's tail when you were 12! The probability of her hiring you may not be so great.

Tip 3: Another place to check is the classified ads in your local paper and also on job-search websites.

ACE THE
APPLICATION

The application is important! It's not a little "questionnaire" or a "no-big-deal" form, as some of our friends have said. Most employers we spoke with emphasized the importance of a neat, complete, well-presented application.

The application represents you. It is often the first major impression the employer gets of you. No spelling errors, no grammar errors. And neatness counts (no crossed-out words). Employers will judge how much effort you put into it. If your application is messy, they might think you're lazy and work in a sloppy, disorganized way.

Tip 1: Bring a pen with you—a nice pen, so you don't risk getting stuck with a leaky one or no pen at all. No pen = not prepared. Not a good first impression!

Tip 2: If possible, take the application form home. There, you can take your time and feel more comfortable when you fill it out. Take an extra blank form with you, so if you make a mistake, you can start again.

Tip 3: If you do take it home, bring the application back in person, and hand it to your future employer or manager.

Tip 4: Before you make a mad dash to fill out your form, be sure to READ each question completely. When we rush, we tend to put our first name where it says "Last Name." It's very important to show the employer you can follow directions correctly. These little things are BIG CLUES to employers.

Tip 5: Make sure you fill out all the blanks in the application. In those blanks that don't apply to you, write N/A ("not applicable").

Tip 6: Never, ever lie on your application. Okay, you went to Costa Rica over the summer and gave your Bible to a local. Don't say you spent your summer as a missionary in Central America! A lie? "Extending the truth"? Either way, it's only a matter of time before our mistruths stab us in the back and we get caught red-handed.

Tip 7: Attach a picture of yourself to the application, even if they don't ask for one. Pictures are hard to throw away because people perceive them to have value. There's a good chance that your photo will sit on the desk of the person who may hire you. The interviewer will remember you.

Tip 8: Attach your Personal Information Attachment (discussed at the end of chapter), listing your personal and sport achievements, the reasons you want this job, and why the employer needs you.

Application Checklist:

❏ **Do I have my own pen to fill out application?**

❏ **Is my application neat? Is it free of spelling and grammatical errors?**

❏ **Did I read and answer every question? Did I write N/A for questions that don't apply to me?**

❏ **Did I attach both my picture and my Personal Information Attachment (see end of chapter)?**

❏ **Did I personally hand my application to my employer and thank him/her for the opportunity?**

RIDDLE ME THIS: "So, tell me about yourself?" This is an all-too-familiar interview question. How are you going to reply?

Before you even step foot into the interview, you must be aware of some of the most common questions you might be asked, and you must practice how you will answer them. Interviewers will ask, "What experience do you have?" and "Why should I hire you?" They are looking to see how you handle the questions and how you relate to others. With practice, you will eliminate any "ummms" and "uhhhhs" and avoid uneasy pauses and puzzled facial expressions.

An interviewer told us this experience:

Interviewer: "So, tell me about yourself."

Young Girl: "Ummm... well... uhhhhhh... I'm 5'7", about 105 pounds, and I've been told I have very healthy hair. I go to school. I have two goldfish named Bubbles and Goldie—well, I did, but I'm pretty irresponsible so I forgot to feed them. Ummmm, what else? I enjoy going to parties and sleeping in too!"

WOW! Did she get the job? If you answered yes, read this chapter at least five times! The interviewer didn't even let her finish her stunning response. Yeah, a great example of what NOT to do.

No matter how clever you are, by reviewing interview questions and practicing your responses, you will sound even smarter, and your interview will go more smoothly. Your knees may still knock but not as

> **2K TIP**
>
> **THE RECEIVING END.** When someone gives you a compliment, there's no need to blush and say, "Gee, shucks. I don't deserve it." News just in: You DO deserve it! They wouldn't have said anything if you didn't. Instead, simply say, "Thank you."

loudly. Remember, it's not a race to see how fast you can answer the interviewer's questions. If you need to, take a few moments to stop and think about how you are going to answer before you open your mouth. If you don't fully understand the question, don't be afraid to ask the interviewer to clarify it.

COMMON QUESTIONS

Here are some common interview questions that you should be prepared to answer:

>> What experience do you have?
>> Why should I hire you?
>> So, tell me about yourself.
>> What do you think your strengths are?
>> Where do you see yourself in five years?
>> What skills would you bring to this job?
>> How would your friends describe you?
>> How many hours a week are you willing to work?
>> Why do you want to work here?
>> What are your weaknesses?
>> Have you ever been fired from a job? If so, why?
>> Do you have any passions?
>> What kind of student do you think you are?

Don't just read through these questions—be ready to answer them! Even if you aren't asked all of them, you'll be better prepared for the ones you are asked.

"Cool Stuff" you should know:

These helpful pointers will help you have a successful interview, make a good first impression, feel good about your performance, and walk away confident.

>> **Be on time!** In all the phone calls we made to employers, the one thing that kept coming up was punctuality. Be on time, but don't be too early, either.

>> **Remember names**, especially those of the interviewer and the BOSS. This is very important, not to mention impressive.

>> **Cover that tat.** If you wear necklaces, bracelets, or bizarre earrings, leave them at home. If you're applying for a job at a tattoo parlor, body art might be appropriate. Otherwise, hide the tattoos; unless they say sweet stuff like "I love Mom" or "My boss is #1."

>> **Don't ramble.** Be complete in your answers, but don't babble on and on. You will also want to avoid one-word answers like "yes," "no," and "maybe." Use detail without being a broken record.

DO IT RIGHT ... THE FIRST TIME. Why go back and do the same thing again? If you're going to do something, spend the extra effort and save yourself the hassle and frustration of repeating the work later.

>> **Wait for the manager to offer you a chair.** Sounds old-fashioned, but this is not the time to be hip. Let the interviewer sit down before you do. It shows respect.

>> **Sit up straight.** Once you sit, slide to the back of the chair and sit up tall. By doing this, you will look more comfortable as well as confident. Don't play Jell-O and slide down your chair; employers like good posture.

>> **Listen.** Remember what he or she tells you. It could help you in the future, either on the job or in a follow-up interview.

>> **Never look at your watch.** The interview is over when the interviewer says it's over. If it helps, leave your watch at home, or just leave it in your pocket.

>> **Dress appropriately.** Don't wear flip-flop sandals, T-shirts, or casual shorts to the interview. People—especially employers—do judge books by their covers. So present yourself nicely. How do other employees in that company dress? Be clothes-minded! The interviewer will see you before he or she hears you. Make it love at first sight.

>> **Make a great first impression.** Did you know that most employers know whether or not they will hire you in the first ten seconds? That's right. From the time they see you, shake your hand, and lead you into their office, a decision has often been made. If they get a negative impression, it is a lasting one.

>> **Turn small mishaps into tests.** If you encounter an embarrassing moment, such as spilling a glass of water, it doesn't have to ruin your interview. Apologize and stay cool. Everything is a test, including the way you handle an accident.

>> **Try to eliminate "um," "ah," "like," and "you know"** from your sentences. These sound, like, um . . . ah . . . um, like you're uneducated, you know? (That was a joke.)

>> **Personality is one of the most important qualities** for some employers. You have to be upbeat and lively when you walk in to the interview. Don't act shy or be intimidated. This is your moment to shine. Be yourself and relax, but most importantly, be enthusiastic! It will be a great start to becoming the number one applicant!

>> **Say "Thank you!"** When appropriate—and certainly when leaving the interview—thank the interviewer by LAST name: "Thank

you, Ms. Newboss."

At the end of the interview, you will probably have some time to ask questions about the job. Ask a few questions to show that you are interested in the position. Avoid asking about things that were covered during the interview; it could look as if you weren't listening.

Here are a few sample questions you can ask:

>> When are you going to make the decision about whom you're hiring?
>> If I get the job, when will I start?
>> What qualities do I need to succeed at this job?
>> What's your dress code? (If appropriate)

PREPARE TO IMPRESS

Making a good impression and people skills are so important in the interview that we're bringing it up again! The first thing you need to do when you walk into the interview is to shake hands with your potential employer. Forget the "dead fish" handshake here, and think real beefcake, a Chuck Norris karate-power handshake.

Seriously, make it firm but not bone-crushing. A good handshake gives the interviewer a taste of your confidence. Be sure to look the employer in the eye while shaking hands, and keep good

Would you hire this person?

eye contact throughout the interview. Put a nice smile on your face to show you are happy to be there. Become really familiar with the chapters Make a Good Impression and People Skills, because just about anything you do in life will involve other people.

DITCH THE DISTRACTIONS

Leave your nervous habits at home. Nail biting, hair twirling, hand twitching—all such distractions will only hinder your chances of getting the job. These might convince the employer that you are edgy and insecure.

Suggestion: Interlock your fingers on your lap to keep them from wandering. However, if that's still not going to stop your arms and hands from bustin' out into a one-person version of the wave, you're better off sitting on your hands and not scaring away the interviewer.

PRACTICE MAKES PERFECT

Improve interview confidence by videotaping yourself. Ask your friends or family members to play the employer. Many people actually do this because **IT WORKS!**

To get the most out of the experience, watch it twice. First, hit the mute button, and keep an eye on your gestures and body position. Be sure to ask for other people's opinions. They might pick up on something you didn't notice.

The second time, turn the sound on. Listen to your pronunciation. Is it clear and easy to understand? Also, pay attention to the words you use and the order you put them in. Does what you're saying make sense? How is your vocabulary? Would you hire you?

Interview Checklist:

☐ **Prepare for questions you might be asked.**
☐ **Be on time.**
☐ **Remember names.**
☐ **Don't ramble.**
☐ **Listen.**
☐ **Dress nicely.**
☐ **Use confident body language.**
☐ **Say "Thank you!"**
☐ **Don't forget to be yourself.**

HOW TO BE THE "# LAST" APPLICANT

Here is The Loser's List ... the things that will really increase your chances of NOT getting the job. Common sense? Apparently not, because according to some employers that we interviewed, too many people really do these things.

>> Take the interviewer's seat when you walk in.
>> Bring an inappropriate adult magazine to read while you're waiting.

>> Check your watch every few minutes, and ask when the interview will be over.

>> Bring your dog.

>> Talk trash about your last boss and fellow employees.

>> Say, "I'm only doing this for the money."

>> Tell them you can't work if the surf is good, there's a party, or you're just too tired.

>> Show up late while eating a large meatball sub. (Be sure to spill sauce on the carpet.)

THE FOLLOW-UP

The follow-up is very important and can make or break your chances of getting the job if the employer is trying to decide between you and another applicant. One thing that will really stand out is a thank-you letter or a call the day after your interview. We're not talking slimy and schmoozy here, just short and simple:

"Thank you for your time and the opportunity to meet you and interview for this position. I look forward to hearing from you soon."

That's it. Short and simple ... and it will put you miles ahead of most competing applicants. It shows that you want the job, that you're genuinely interested. Don't go overboard though; know when enough is enough and where to draw the line between kindness and kissing up.

KEEPING THE JOB

"Wahoo! I got the job!" Good for you! But don't get too comfortable. You're only halfway there. The manager will watch to see if your work ethic backs up your resume, your application, and your responses in the interview.

Everything you do will be evaluated. Once you have the job, the manager will watch you to see if you:

>> Crack under pressure
>> Follow directions
>> Get along with the other staff
>> Deal with customers well
>> Are reliable, honest, and hardworking

Tip 1: Don't be afraid to do more than you are asked to do. Be self-motivated. Sitting and waiting for a customer to come in won't help you or the business. If you don't know much about your field of work, cruise around the shop/office/factory, pick up products or brochures, and learn about the items you're selling. If you don't understand something, ask a fellow employee for help, but never pretend you know when you don't. Try to do your work better than you think it needs to be done—even if you think no one is looking. Eventually they will. Heck, in time, it might earn you that raise you wanted.

Tip 2: Now is also the time to put those people skills to use. Your job will last longer if you are nice and patient with fellow employees and helpful to customers. If you feel your people skills aren't very good, there is only one thing you can do: Practice. On-the-job-training is great, but you need to apply these skills to everyone, at all times.

Tip 3: Since technology plays a major role in getting a job these days, knowing how to use a computer will make you more valuable and versatile (employers like that). Note: If you are unfamiliar with the equipment you are expected to use, be sure to ASK! Learn everything you can about it. Being familiar with the tools will make you more efficient.

THE DIFFERENCE

When it's a toss-up between applicants, the little extra effort you put in might make the difference. We suggest attaching a Personal Information form similar to the one on the right to your job application. For a printable copy, go to our website: www.coolstuffmedia.com. Who knows ... it might be what separates you from the next person.

THE WRAP

Follow the steps in this chapter, and you will increase your chances of getting the job you want! To ace your chances, refer back to this information. Once just ain't enough! Good luck!

The Personal Information Attachment

Name: _____

Date: _____ **Age:** _____

Position applied for: _____

_____

*PHOTO

Why I want this job: You might include: specific interests, location, earn money for college, come here all the time, love bikes, love surfing, enjoy working with people, want to learn (about animals, about motorcycles, how to cook, etc.).

Why you want me for this job: You might include: I'm efficient, punctual, hardworking, enthusiastic, a quick learner, etc.

What I can do for you: You might include: How you'll make the customers happy, brighten up the liveliness of the workplace, etc.

Personal achievements:
You might include: Academic, athletic, work accomplishments, community service, etc.

My "To Do" List:

- ❑ "Want" to get a job.
- ❑ Tell people I'm looking for a job (if you really are). Use my contacts too.
- ❑ Find a job I like.
- ❑ Fill out and present the application the best I can.
- ❑ Practice my interviewing skills before the actual interview.
- ❑ Use my body language to my advantage.
- ❑ Know what I should not do in an interview, and avoid these negatives.
- ❑ Follow up after the application or interview.
- ❑ Use my people skills to keep the job.
- ❑ Go the extra mile, and attach the Personal Information sheet to my application.
- ❑ Look forward to making my own money!

"Cool Stuff" I need to take note of:

_____

_____

_____

_____

_____

_____

_____

_____

_____

"B. Y. O. B." 06

Do what you love,
love what you do . . .
and get paid for it!

BE YOUR OWN BOSS

No, B.Y.O.B. does not mean "Bring Your Own Beer." Sorry! Even though it has nothing to do with beer, this chapter is related to partying—a lifetime party, in fact!

B.Y.O.B. means "Be Your Own Boss." Do you want to be in charge of your life and make your own money? If working for someone else just isn't your thing and you'd rather be your own boss, then this chapter is for you! If you've ever wanted to own a business, there's never been a better time.

Kent: When my brother and I moved to Tauranga, New Zealand, we wanted to surf and skimboard at the beach near our house. Problem: We couldn't find the type of skimboard we wanted. We must have checked about 15 surf shops before realizing they were not sold in our area. Bummer! Or is it good news? Hmmm ... Was this our opportunity to become self-employed and be our own bosses? It was!

At ages 14 and 15, we researched different marine plywoods, shapes, sizes, and resins, and we started a skateboard and skimboard business. Our company, "Reactor Board Technology," produced two skimboard models that met retail standards.

We turned our garage into a small workshop, formed an assembly line, and sold our boards to surf shops in New Zealand, Australia, Hawaii, and California. (Okay, we sold only a few boards overseas, but we wanted to sound "international.")

Along the way, we learned how to work with retail shops,

form deals, and communicate with business professionals. The lessons we learned were invaluable, but an unsuspected bonus was the freedom we created for ourselves. Having freedom, we discovered, was one key reason people like working for themselves! So that's why people want to be their own boss ...

WHY SHOULD I BE MY OWN BOSS?

Owning a business brings a whole new set of challenges and experiences. Maybe you should—and maybe you should not—be your own boss. The choice is yours, but like every important choice you make, your decision requires some thinking, a look at the pros and cons. In this case, you might consider how you value money, your time, your freedom, your confidence, your opportunities.

Your money: Anyone who has a choice won't choose minimum wage or hourly pay. No way! Entrepreneurs have some control over how much money they make.

WOULDN'T IT BE COOL TO MAKE WHAT YOU KNOW YOU ARE WORTH INSTEAD OF WHAT THE STORE MANAGER THINKS YOU ARE WORTH?

When you own the business, your personal effort determines your income. As a result, you can earn enough cash to buy a sweet car, the clothes you want, CDs, or whatever else you want. Of course, if you'd rather wait and save up all that money you're making by stocking shelves or sweeping warehouses for someone else ... well, that's up to you.

Your time: If you're self-employed, you can decide when you want to work and for how long. You can work around your ideal schedule, not what's best for your boss. Do what you want, when you want. This doesn't mean you're on permanent vacation. In fact, it's usually the opposite. Business owners, as a rule, work long and hard hours. But hey, if you are doing what you love, it's not really "work." The point is that you are the one in charge of your own work hours.

Your freedom and independence: Tired of being told what to do? Well, when you are the boss, you call the shots. Every decision is yours.

Your confidence: Do you like the natural high of doing what you want? Working for yourself gives you that feeling. It builds confidence, which will only help you in all other parts of life.

Your opportunities: Many opportunities arise when you're an entrepreneur. Here are just a few:

>> You get the chance to learn how to run a business, to see what works and what doesn't. That knowledge is invaluable.

>> You'll get the chance to meet all sorts of successful people—people who love to help entrepreneurs like you. Their tips and their help will help you excel even further.

>> You'll better your chances of being accepted into a university. Running your own business is quite an accomplishment, and it looks great on a resume. College admission boards will be impressed that you have the skills, passion, and experience of an entrepreneur. Often these skills can outweigh someone who has straight A's but no "real world" understanding and knowledge.

>> You'll learn how to manage money. Now that's priceless knowledge.

>> You'll discover how to get along with others, create deals, and make new friendships.

>> You'll improve your selling and organizational skills, skills that will help you succeed in life.

Now that's a lot of opportunities! Just imagine how much your personal and professional lives could change by working for yourself.

AM I AN ENTREPRENEUR?

Not everyone is an entrepreneur. But one thing is for sure: Most people are, and they don't even realize it. Entrepreneurship is more an attitude than a skill or a profession. It's a decision to look for opportunities and make something out of them.

Do you have a hobby? What do you enjoy doing? If you like to do more than sitting on the couch, twiddling your thumbs, and staring into space, then you're in luck.

Do you like building stuff? Why not make and sell mailboxes or birdhouses? If your passion is computers, send out flyers telling your neighbors that you'll fix or set up their computers. The computer market is huge. This is just one example of how to make some serious coin.

Got other ideas? What do you like doing? What are the possibilities of taking the next step and creating some income while being your own boss?

Kent: *I've always been interested in drawing and art. I wasn't always good at it, but because it was my passion and I worked hard at it, my skills improved. The important thing is that I loved it.*

When Kyle and I started our company, Reactor Board Technology, I did all the advertising, board graphics, logos, etc. Guess what? I kept getting better at it. When I was 16, I went to the local surfboard shaper and made a deal with them. First, I whipped up a business card on the computer to look professional, brought my written proposal, and offered to design a new corporate logo for the shaper in return for a custom-made surfboard. After a little bargaining, we had a deal.

I scored a custom surfboard worth $600 for doing something I loved to do anyway! I was stoked! Soon, I started visiting local swim clubs, surf clubs, and sports teams and started doing designs for them. What a cool feeling when you work for yourself.

I CAN'T DO THAT

If you think you can't, you're right. You're capable of doing only what you think you can do. Don't look for reasons why you can't do something. *Excuses are plentiful! And if you can't find your own, there are plenty of people who will lend you some of theirs! If you are looking, there will always be reasons why something can't be done.*

Instead, turn the phrase "I can't do that" into "How can I do that?" Take the "t" out of *can't*. Heck, nothing worthwhile happens by chance. You have to work for the good stuff! Anything is possible as long as you truly believe it.

WHAT DO I NEED TO BE AN ENTREPRENEUR?

Entrepreneurs have certain skills that separate them from the rest of the crowd. And if you are missing a key skill, you can develop it. We're not talking about superhuman powers you are given at birth. In fact, entrepreneurs are not born with all these qualities. But, they do have one thing in common: the desire to become an entrepreneur.

You can develop any of the following skills IF you have the desire. Note that even if you don't want to be an entrepreneur, developing these abilities will help you in all parts of your life!

WHAT ARE YOUR DREAMS?

THE BIGGEST ADVENTURE YOU CAN EVER TAKE IS TO LIVE THE LIFE OF YOUR DREAMS.

—Oprah Winfrey

Gotta have dreams, gotta have vision. Very important! Not the vision to pass an eye exam, but the vision that allows you to see things that don't exist yet, like your business and your opportunities. You can't physically see them, but you can imagine their potential and see beyond the present time, like the vision you

have for an exciting party next weekend or a date tomorrow night—that kind of vision. That's why it is important to venture into an area you really like.

YES, BUT AM I CREATIVE ENOUGH?

Everybody has creativity, but most of us don't give ourselves credit for having any. Flash back to when you were a little kid, running around and pretending you were a superhero (or a cowboy) and the playground (or your kitchen) was your own universe. Do you remember how real it all was through your eyes?

Still not convinced you're creative? Well, what about all those stories for not turning in your homework or those excuses for being late for class? See? We told you you were creative!

Yes, everyone has creativity—and you certainly do. It's just a matter of remembering you do and building on this skill after childhood.

YA GOTTA HAVE FAITH

An entrepreneur needs confidence. Faith in yourself and in your actions is a must. Remember that being your own boss will increase your confidence too. Stand strong next to your actions and business.

NOW, ABOUT YOUR WILLPOWER

LACK OF WILLPOWER HAS CAUSED MORE FAILURE THAN LACK OF INTELLIGENCE OR ABILITY.

—*Flower A. Newhouse*

Whether you like it or not, you will face difficult times. If you're a true entrepreneur, you'll live the dream of "The Little Engine That Could" and finish what you started. Winston Churchill, the late great prime minister of England, once said:

IF YOU'RE GOING THROUGH HELL, KEEP GOING.

He's exactly right. These are the times when your true colors shine. It is easy to be happy and relaxed when all is well, but a champion will continue to shine through the good and the bad.

Being flaky or indecisive will get you nowhere. Live up to your game plan, and stick to it until you've reached your goal. It is too easy to lose interest in all the work and commitment. You know what helped us the most with Reactor, our skim board company? We always kept the rewards in mind when we found it hard to continue. We soon learned that the rewards always outweighed the sacrifices.

DISCIPLINE
MEANS FREEDOM

We all grew up with someone pushing our stroller, but that time is now over (it IS over, right?). Someone won't always be there to push you when times get tough. All of us must learn to pick ourselves up during the tough times, and that ability only comes from within ourselves. It is undoubtedly one of the best traits we can develop.

Do you respect people who give their word and then do as they promised? People who set a schedule and stick to it? That's discipline. At the other end are those annoying people who say "I'll call you tomorrow" or "I'll have the project finished by Tuesday." All talk, no action. What kind of person do you want to be?

It's that simple. When you say you're going to have a project done by a certain time, ***then do it!*** You can't afford to be flaky in business. It's the guaranteed best way to lose customers, clients, money, and your business. The good news is that discipline is a muscle. You can develop it with willingness. Just make an effort to do what you say. To make sure your word means something to others, you must first make sure it means something to YOU.

HOCUS FOCUS

Achieving your goals is kind of like target shooting. You have to concentrate and focus on the bull's-eye if you want to hit it.

The same holds true for reaching your goals. You must focus on them if you want to reach them. Your ability to focus will save you a lot of time!

Kyle: *Each time Kent and I started a business, we were bombarded with other distractions—school, sports, surfing, and ... parties. It wasn't always easy to finish what we started, because our attention was being pulled in so many different directions. We learned quickly: If you can't concentrate on your target, you will never hit it.*

BE THE BEST

Top athletes are competitive. They have to be. They have to push themselves and their potential to the limit to achieve the extraordinary. Some people see competitiveness as an annoying or negative trait, but just like sports, competitiveness in the entrepreneurial world is critical to success.

Take a quick look at the companies out there today. Quiksilver, for example, has to compete against Billabong, Ripcurl, Rusty, Hurley, etc. McDonald's competes against Burger King, Wendy's, etc. Ford competes against Chevrolet, Honda, Toyota, VW, etc. Competition is what business is all about! As in the sports world, in the business world you must have enough competitiveness to contend with and stand up to your competition. Successful entrepreneurs push themselves and their businesses to the limit.

"PLAYS WELL WITH OTHERS"

Every business involves others. Who would you sell your goods or services to? Who would sell them for you? This means you must be able to get along with others, develop professional relationships, keep friendships, and create new ones. Here we go again; we're back to making a good impression and polishing those people skills. You never know who might be a future customer. The more people who like you, the better off

BE A LEADER

Entrepreneurs are leaders, not followers. They have the ability to blaze their own path with confidence and leadership. It's good to consider advice from others, but ultimately entrepreneurs will call the shots.

GET EXCITED!

ENTHUSIASM IS THE SMALL SPARK THAT MARKS THE DIFFERENCE BETWEEN THE LEADERS IN EVERY ACTIVITY AND THE SLACKERS WHO PUT IN JUST ENOUGH EFFORT TO GET BY.
—*Unknown*

Love what you do, do what you love. Enthusiasm is the fuel for success. When you're excited about what you're doing, you'll be more successful. Drive and perseverance feed off your enthusiasm. When you're excited, other people get excited too. Develop a passion for what you're doing, and success is just around the corner.

BE PENNY-WISE

A PENNY SAVED IS A PENNY EARNED.
—*Benjamin Franklin*

A lot of successful business people have learned this strategy: As an entrepreneur, you have to spend money wisely and reinvest it whenever you can. You don't need to be a Scrooge in order to be penny-wise. Just keep an eye on what you spend money on and how you distribute your income.

BE PRODUCTIVE

Most people complain about never having enough time. The truth is, there isn't much time! But guess what? No one has more than you do: a 24-hour day and a 168-hour week. It's how you use the time that matters.

> *"Cool Stuff"*
>
> BEING "BUSY" AND BEING "PRODUCTIVE" ARE TWO DIFFERENT THINGS.

Make a habit to "GET THINGS DONE!" Use your time wisely.

The Entrepreneur's Checklist:

- ❏ Make my dream a reality.
- ❏ Think "out of the box"and think unconventionally.
- ❏ Believe in myself and what I'm doing!
- ❏ Expect hard times, but always keep the rewards in mind.
- ❏ Live up to my word.
- ❏ Be competitive, and strive to be the best I can.
- ❏ Treat others the way I want to be treated.
- ❏ Be the leader, and blaze my own paths.
- ❏ Be enthusiastic about what I do!
- ❏ Use my money wisely.
- ❏ Always be willing to adapt to changing situations & markets.
- ❏ Use my time wisely.

PRACTICE
FLEXIBILITY

If you can touch your toes, great! But that's not the kind of flexibility we're talking about here. We're talking about the ability to adapt to changing situations, conditions, and markets. Like it or not, nothing stays the same forever. Unless you're selling collectables, you'll have to change your products, services, and ideas to suit the current demand.

"BUT WHAT SHOULD I DO?"

If you can't come up with a business idea right away, don't sweat it. For now, focus on the stuff you love doing. What are your hobbies? What are your passions? How can you turn your hobby or passion into a job opportunity?

Remember: Be professional, research the best possible techniques for doing a job, check liabilities, and check local government agencies regarding permits, etc.

Here is a list of some jobs to get your mind thinking about what you can do to Be Your Own Boss!

>> Wash windows: This worked really well for us. Our window-washing company was called "Mario & Squeegee Bros." We went door to door in uniforms, asking homeowners and businesses if they would like their windows cleaned. We gave them free quotes (our charges to

do the job) and scheduled them in for the time that suited us best. We earned quite a few bucks, became very good at window-washing, and still had time for school, sports, and hanging out with friends.

>> Wash cars: Do cars stay clean forever? Of course not. It's an infinite market with tons of business available, including lots of repeat business. Everyone wants a clean car, but does everyone have the time? Do the math: If you make $10 a car and wash ten cars (two cars an hour), that's $100 or $20 an hour! Not bad, huh? (You won't get that flipping burgers.) If you can wash cars well and fast, then here's your business. Just walk around your neighborhood (or any other neighborhood), and ask people.

>> Housesit: Friends and neighbors leaving town? Ask them if you can watch their house. Pick up their newspapers and their mail, mow their lawn, water their plants, and walk the dog.

>> Clean gutters: Naturally, gutters fill with leaves and other stuff that clogs them and stops the draining. Equipment: A lightweight ladder, a bucket, and gloves. Just walk from house to house,

WORK IT. Let's face it ... there are times when we get buried with work. And usually the first thing a lot of people overlook is exercise. Working out, though, gives us more energy to do the things we have to do better and more efficiently.

and ask politely. In the fall, there is almost no limit to the business you can get.

>> Wash and groom pets: Love animals? Then this job has your name on it! All you need is pet shampoo, a wash bin, combs, brushes, and old towels.

>> Petsit: If you love animals, it will seem like you're getting paid to have fun! Offer to take care of your friends' pets when they go on vacation. You can feed 'em, wash 'em, walk 'em, and watch 'em.

And stress the fact that their beloved Rover will be with you rather than in an ugly, uncaring, lonely, loud, dirty kennel. Ugh!

>> **Mow lawns:** Got a lawn mower? Every lawn must be mowed, so if you have a lawn mower, you're set. With a little gas and some comfortable shoes, wander around your neighborhood, find some overgrown lawns, knock on the door, cut a deal, and rake in the bucks. And work on your tan while you mow!

>> **Babysit:** Tell all the parents you know that you're open for business. Encourage them to go out for the night, because you can be there to watch the kids. After all, they know you're reliable!

>> **Wax cars, boats, etc.:** Pack some good auto wax and a few rags, and start talking to people with cars, boats, patio furniture, planes, etc. Ask if they want their vehicles looking good. Don't overlook all those cars in office parking lots.

>> **Cook:** Are you quite a chef? Then cook! If your family has a secret recipe "everyone just loves," use it to make a few bucks. Cook up a few specialties, and throw a bake sale wherever you can. (And don't eat all the profits.) Good on the BBQ? If you know people who are having a party, offer to work your magic on the grill while they kick back and enjoy themselves.

>> **Do craft work:** Are you creative, good with your hands, or just love making stuff? Use your skills to build birdhouses, shoe racks, mailboxes, or whatever you can create. Then sell them to neighbors and friends.

Are you beginning to see how many ways there to make money quickly and easily? Here are a few more ...

>> **Clean houses:** Are you the organized, neat, and tidy type? If so, sell your skills to other people. Offer to clean houses for a price you think is right.

>> Be a personal assistant: A lot of working people are too busy to run errands, pick up and drop off kids, fix things, clean the yard, tidy up the house, or assemble that new barbecue. Talk to people who seem really busy. Ask your parents if they know anyone who might want a personal assistant. Nowadays, this is a thriving business.

>> Tutor others: So you're great in math? English? History? Tutor other students ... show them your tricks for mastering the subject. Tutors can make a lot of money. So ... who could use your help?

>> Buy an asset and put it to work for you: Buy a power washer to clean driveways, walkways, outside furniture, house siding, etc. The first few jobs will pay for the equipment, and after that, your income will be pure profit. Hmmm ...

2K TIP

'WHAT'S COOKIN'? Learning how to cook is invaluable. We're all going to have to learn some day. Pick up some tips from Mom or Dad in the kitchen ... it might even land you a second date.

>> Design websites: Do you like computers and surfing the Internet? Do you have a touch of creativity? Know how to develop websites and use design programs? Well, sell your skills! Create your own website, and advertise your business. People need you!

>> Be a gardener/landscaper: Every yard needs maintenance. Clip hedges, pick up leaves, get rid of weeds. If you have a creative flair for landscaping, then suggest new ideas and layouts for your customers' yards. Go for it!

>> Clean garages: Stop laughing! It's NOT stupid! How many people do you know with messy garages? (Answer: All of 'em.) All people want their garages organized, but no one has the time to do it. Come up with a price you think is right. Don't forget to send flyers all over your neighborhood!

YOUR IDEA IS...?

Don't be fooled. Your idea does not need to be new and revolutionary. You can take an old idea and market it in different ways or slightly change it to suit today's style.

Of course, if you do have your own new idea, great! A piece of advice: Never wait for someone to tell you it's a good idea! Go for it! Being an entrepreneur is all about independence. Believe in yourself and especially your ideas. Sometimes you must simply listen to yourself and not others, not even your parents. You are the one who knows what's hot and what's not. Take the chance! Dare to be different.

BUT HOW DO I GET WORK?

Talk a lot: Tell everyone about your business, even people you know cannot use your product or service, because they will know others who can. Tell everyone, and be sure to ask who they know who might be interested. Network!

Walk a lot: Start walking door-to-door and talking to people. Explain who you are and what you're doing.

>> If they say "YES": Good job. You're in! Do your best work. Be sure to thank them when you are finished.

>> If they say "NO": That's okay. Not everyone's going to be interested, but make sure you're polite and say "thanks" no matter what. Don't let the "NOs" get you down. Going door-to-door can be tough, but it will pay off. (continued on page 126)

Your door-to-door checklist:

❏ **Dress for success.** You don't need a suit or a fancy dress, but you must look good.

❏ **Smile!**

❏ **Look people in the eye.**

❏ **Tell them your name.** If you're a student, say so.

❏ **Say something nice** whenever it's genuine. For example, if you see something you like about their house, compliment them. Who doesn't like genuine comments?

❏ **Speak clearly.** They're not going to buy your product or services if they can't understand what you are saying or selling.

❏ **Describe what you're doing.** If you are starting a business, let them know.

❏ **Be concise.** Whatever you do, don't ramble. No one likes to stand at the door and listen to someone's life story.

Expect to hear "no" often. Remember, every "no" is someone who now knows you are open for business. Whenever people turn you down, ask them who they know that might be able to use your services!

>> *Advertise with flyers:* Make flyers, and start walking around the neighborhood. Drop them on doorsteps, or give them to people. Caution: It's illegal to stick them in mailboxes! If you can, make door hangers—flyers you can attach to doorknobs. So if your business has commercial promise (for example, if you're washing windows), pass out flyers to commercial shops and industrial buildings. That's what we did, and it worked well.

>> *More about flyers:* Designing your flyer is very important. Remember, your flyer speaks for you, so you want it to be easy to read and persuasive. Convince them your service or product is worth buying!

Here is an example of a flyer we used for Mario & Squeegee Bros., our window-washing company:

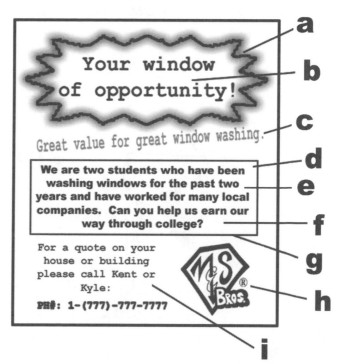

Flyer tips:

>> **a.** Create a design that stands out and grabs attention right away.

>> **b.** Come up with a clever heading.

>> **c.** Make it clear and easy to tell exactly what you're offering. (We put our key sentence at an angle to grab attention as well as break up all the other writing.)

>> **d.** Sell them. Tell them in as few words as possible why they should hire you! If you're a student, then tell them. People like to help students.

>> **e.** If you have some experience or achievements related to what you're doing, let them know. It shows you can do the job well.

>> **f.** Ask a question that involves them. "Can you help me?" It forces people to start thinking about how they can contribute.

>> **g.** One way to break up all the writing is to use boxes. Boxes will make your flyer clearer and easier to read.

>> **h.** Create a logo to make your business look more professional. (Note the M&S logo on our flyer.)

>> **i.** Politely ask them to call you if they are interested. And don't forget to include your number on the flyer!

>> **One more step:** Proofread your flyer. Then ask others to read it before you distribute it out to the public! A simple spelling mistake can make your potential customers doubt your intelligence and decide not to use your business.

>> **Be creative (revisited):** Any other ways to market your product or service? For example, if you're making birdhouses, visit your local garden shop, show them what you're making, and ask if you

can hang one somewhere in the store with a sign. On your sign, be sure to indicate that it is locally made, the price, and any cool features. The possibilities are endless. Offer to split the profits with the store for using their premises and sharing their customers. Start thinking, and the ideas will come.

WORDS OF WISDOM

Never be afraid to ask or call anyone for advice. Adults, parents, and other entrepreneurs are untapped resources. If you're polite and sincere, it will be hard for them to turn you down. When someone helps you, keep his or her name and number, and stay in touch. Let them know whenever their advice worked or their tips paid off. These people are invaluable; if they helped you once, they may be able to help you again.

Anytime you can learn from another's experience, it is to your benefit. Why make mistakes others have already made? And learning from their successes is just as important.

BE A PRIVATE EYE

Investigate your idea before you start. There is usually more to it than meets the eye. We learned the hard way ... several times.

When we started Reactor Board Technology, we assumed we knew what materials would work best for our skim boards and spent a lot of money on special resins, fiberglass, materials, etc. When we found the bottoms of the boards were wearing out really fast, we knew something was wrong. We finally realized we needed to do more research. It turned out we bought and used the wrong resin. Time to cut our losses and learn from our mistake.

And it was a very expensive mistake. We did the research in advance, but we did not do enough. Our lesson was expensive. However, it has saved us a lot of money and frustration since then.

BUSINESS: AGAIN AND AGAIN AND ...

Repeat business ... the very words make us smile! Repeat business can be BIG money. If you're washing someone's car, ask them when they would like you to return—every week? Every two weeks? Regular customers mean regular income. Of course, *always ask for referrals!*

KEEP TRACK OF OF YOUR BIZ

If you're organized, you'll have more fun and make more money. Believe us on this one; it's true. We learned the hard way but want to save you from the same frustration.

Kyle: When we started Reactor, we didn't do a very good job of tracking our sales. It blew up in our face when we discovered there were several people who owed us money. We couldn't contact three of them, because we failed to record their correct contact information. As a result, we experienced unnecessary frustration and lost a couple hundred dollars. Lesson: Be organized!

Here is a quick checklist of the things you should consider when managing your business:

>> **1. Get an invoice book to track:**
    a. When you did the job
    b. The date you got paid
    c. How much you made
    d. Customer contact information

>> **2. Create a folder at home to store all your records. Make sure to include:**
    a. Where you worked
    b. Who you worked for
    c. Miscellaneous job comments

>> **3. Write down names, addresses, directions, phone numbers, and all other details. This is your client list for future business.**

THE WRAP

When you are your own boss, anything is possible. This is your chance to show others what you're really made of—and at the same time, prove it to yourself!

If you're a teenager and still in school or living at home, you can start your business just for the fun of doing it! If you don't need the income for food and rent, then you have the freedom to take risks. And if your parents are at your side to help you, you can take bigger risks. If you're not worried about your next meal, you won't lose sleep over a bad decision. Go with your gut feeling, and be confident! There's no job better than B.Y.O.B.!

No, this isn't "everything you need to know" to start and manage your own business. That will be in one of our following books. We'll discuss specific tips and detailed information to successfully set up and run your own company. Be on the lookout for it!

(No, this is not shameless advertising ... it's just a plug for our upcoming book, so be quiet.)

My "To Do" List!

❑ Start dreaming and come up with my business idea.
(Remember: It doesn't have to be the first idea.)
❑ Remove all my doubts about becoming my own boss.
❑ Strap on my shoes, and "walk a lot."
❑ Get ready to "talk a lot." Let others know what I'm doing.
❑ Advertise by flyers or any other creative way.
❑ Seek other people's advice.
❑ Research my market and my product or service before I start.
❑ Work at getting repeat business and referrals from my customers.
❑ Keep track of my business records.
❑ Go for it!

Managing 07
the Green

Why isn't everyone
a millionaire?

MANAGING THE GREEN

> THE FIRST RULE TO BECOMING WEALTHY
> IS NOT TO LOSE MONEY. THE SECOND
> RULE IS NOT TO FORGET THE FIRST RULE.
>
> —Warren Buffet

Want a sweet car or a dream house? Wake up, and pay attention! This isn't going to be your usual boring lecture about putting money in a piggy bank!

Now that you've got a job (or at least some money to manage), you should know what to do with it and how to make your money work for you. Piggy banks and hoarding are things of the past. You can't expect to get any richer by stuffin' your dough under a mattress. The problem, however, is that people make a lot of excuses when it comes time to invest. For instance:

>> I'm too young. (That's not going to work.)
>> It's too hard. (Yeah, right ...)
>> I don't need to. (Living in la-la land?)

Now some truths: It's never too early to invest, it's not difficult, and it's definitely worth it! Controlling your money empowers you in all areas of your life!

LET'S GET SOMETHING STRAIGHT

THE Rule: **Pay yourself first!** It may seem a little selfish, but if you don't, you'll never be financially set. This means you take the first 10% (or more—remember, it's YOUR business, Boss!) of what you earn and invest it right away.

> MONEY NEVER SEEN CANNOT BE MISSED.

This method has been used since ancient times and has always paid off:

> GOLD COMETH GLADLY AND IN INCREASING QUANTITY TO ANY MAN WHO WILL PUT BY NOT LESS THAN ONE-TENTH OF HIS EARNINGS TO CREATE AN ESTATE FOR HIS FUTURE ...
>
> —George Clason

Too hard? Try this question first: Do you want to adjust your habits a little bit, or do you prefer digging for spare change in couches and phone booths? How do you want to live for the rest of your life?

Congratulations! You're still reading, so you've answered correctly. Now is the best time to get your money habits right. Make the decision to "upgrade" your lifestyle. If you don't make your money work for you, no one else will.

GET YOUR MONEY TO WORK FOR YOU

Do you want to work for your money or have your money work for you? Hmmmm ... that's a hard one. Get your money to earn you more money by investing. Remember: When we say, "Have your money work for you," we don't mean that you can sit there in front of the TV sipping a cold one, while Mr. Franklin (yeah, the face on your $100 bill) is out there raking the leaves.

The goal is to make money your slave, not your boss. The key to that goal is making the right investments, investments that will give you a return on your money.

Q: What's a "return"?

A: It's the money you earn *in addition to the money you invested.*

You can get a return from all sorts of investments: bank accounts, bonds, CDs, stocks, mutual funds, minerals, and when you have enough money, real estate. For example, let's say you put $1,000 in a savings account and that savings bank pays 5% interest a year. After one full year in the bank, your $1,000 investment will have earned $50—that's your "return." Basically, the lower the risk, the lower the return. Savings banks are considered very safe (thus the low return). We'll discuss return and risk in greater detail in later chapters.

Now, some people consider every large expense an "investment." Not true! Be aware of how much money you spend on things that don't hold their value, because this is when you will lose money. For example, the instant you buy a computer, it has almost no resale value. Computers are guaranteed to be state-of-the-art for about five days! After that, it's old. Computers and cars are necessities, not investments (unless the car is a classic).

Making your money work for you is an extremely valuable skill. The sooner you learn to make returns from good investments, the sooner you'll retire.

PRIORITIZE
PRIORITIZE

There's a not-so-secret ingredient to becoming financially free that all wealthy people know about. Here it is: **Make money a priority.** A priority ... not your sole purpose for living and not your god.

If money becomes your primary focus, the only guarantee is unhappiness. We don't want that. Money is important, but it doesn't make the world go around. Take the wisdom of playwright Henrik Ibsen into consideration:

> MONEY MAY BE THE HUSK OF MANY THINGS, BUT NOT THE KERNEL. IT BRINGS YOU FOOD, BUT NOT APPETITE; MEDICINE, BUT NOT HEALTH; ACQUAINTANCES, BUT NOT FRIENDS; SERVANTS BUT NOT LOYALTY; DAYS OF JOY, BUT NOT PEACE OR HAPPINESS.

Money is the root of all evil. Not true! But love of money is. There is a fine line of separation: If you never think about money or simply assume that somehow, some way, you'll make it big, you'll never be financially free. But you will become wealthy if you think about money, find clever (yet lawful) ways to get it, learn how to invest it wisely, and most of all, have fun getting it.

"Cool Stuff"

DON'T MAKE MONEY TO BE HAPPY.
BE HAPPY TO MAKE MONEY.

THE LITTLE THINGS
ADD UP

Our friend considered herself a good saver. She'd rarely go shopping and seriously thought about any purchase over five bucks. One day, we noticed that she always had a bottle of water or soda in her hand. When we asked, she said she bought "about two a day but only on weekdays. They're only a dollar."

It doesn't take a math genius to figure out that's $40 a month and a whopping $480 a year—just on water and soda!!! Today she fills her own bottles at home ... and pockets the extra $480.

Yes, she failed to keep track of the little things. Each time we interviewed financially successful people, we heard the same quote:

"Cool Stuff"

TAKE CARE OF YOUR PENNIES AND YOUR
DOLLARS WILL TAKE CARE OF THEMSELVES.

It's the little habits you create and the little things you spend money on that add up and make a big difference. If you have the discipline to control both, you'll be financially ahead of most people.

BEFORE YOU BUST
YOUR WALLET OUT

> **"Cool Stuff"**
> PEOPLE TEND TO SPEND MONEY ON THINGS THEY DON'T NEED TO IMPRESS PEOPLE THEY DON'T LIKE.

Are the things you buy "needs" or "wants"? Needs, of course, include water, food, and (for some) deodorant. Wants are things you can survive without: a Gucci wristwatch, an expensive car, a knockout sound system. Before you make a major purchase (or any purchase, for that matter), ask yourself these questions:

Do I really *need* this? Can I survive without this?
Y ❑ N ❑
Is the price reasonable?
Y ❑ N ❑
Can I get a substitute for less?
Y ❑ N ❑
Will I regret this purchase next week?
Y ❑ N ❑

Whenever you're spending money, make sure you're in your rational mindset, not an emotional one. When you're excited, it's easy to make bad decisions. We've found one of the best ways to avoid buying something you might regret is to create a cooling-down period.

Before you bust out your wallet, stop. Use the *"Cool Stuff"* law of put-it-on-the-backburner. It's not complicated: Just wait at least 72 hours before making a big decision. Why? You might find in a couple days that you no longer want what you were going to buy. **A great way to get rich is not to spend.**

YOU HAVE TO GIVE
BEFORE YOU GET

Y ou don't get a tree unless you plant a seed. It's the same with investing. You'll never become rich unless you plant your money into a worthwhile investment. The more time that passes, the more your money will grow ... just like a tree.

Don't expect someone to give you money. It won't happen! Your dreams will come true only from your own sacrifices. For two summers, we sacrificed TONS of time we could have had hanging out with friends and going to the beach in order to finish this book. But giving our time and effort has contributed to getting the life we want.

In other words, you give up some things now to make things easier (or better) later on. To save more money, you might go to fewer movies and eat out less often. This does not mean you should turn into a troll, never leave your room, and live in fear of spending a penny (or two) if you step outside the door. Don't be afraid to use your money to have fun. Just be ready to sacrifice a little now in order to create a (much) better future.

OPPORTUNITY COST

Whether it's buying a new stereo or an expensive outfit, each choice you make has an opportunity cost. Listen as Jamie explains ...

Jamie: *For ten years, my parents put one thousand dollars into a savings account for me. When I turned eighteen, it was mine to spend, save, or invest as I wished. My parents hoped by that age, I'd be able to use the money wisely.*

As soon as my eighteenth birthday rolled around, my uncle offered me the opportunity to take the money and invest with him in a rental house he was purchasing. However, for the last few years, I had my heart set on a red Ford Mustang. It was a hard choice for me.

In the end, I chose the car because it gave me immediate freedom to go wherever I needed to go without waiting or asking someone for a ride. The rental property would have tied my money up for a long time. Now, years later, the car is gone, and so is the money.

My uncle's investment in the rental property has more than doubled. I would have had over twenty thousand dollars today if I had better evaluated the real opportunity cost of buying the Mustang.

So, opportunity cost means that when you make one choice, you're giving up another alternative. Essentially Jamie had to choose between pleasure now or delayed gratification. Opportunity cost doesn't need to be an expensive decision, like Jamie's. It can be as simple as choosing to see a movie or getting a summer job instead of just laxing out the entire time.

Any decision that leaves you with two or more choices is an example of opportunity cost. What decision contributes to the life you want?

TOO GOOD TO BE TRUE

When a deal sounds too good to be true, it probably is. Play detective for a while. Investigate and check things out. If it's a scam, get out! But if it's legitimate (don't count on it), you certainly don't want to miss out. In the end, it's your call.

Kyle: *One of our best friends came to visit us while we were living in New Zealand. To protect his innocence, we'll call him David (even though his name is John). He learned an important lesson about jumping into a situation that sounds a little too good to be true.*

It was a hot summer day and the three of us—Kent, David (John), and I—were walking around our property. As we were approaching the top paddock where we kept our three cows, David (John) saw a thin orange wire surrounding the area the cows occupied.

As your typical California farmboy (yeah right), he asked what it was. Kent and I explained to him that it was a "hot wire" or electric fence that kept the cows from wandering around and eating our neighbor's garden. Jokingly, we made him a deal. We told David (John) we'd give him twenty bucks if he peed on the wire. Before he got any ideas, we straight up told him that he'd get a shock ... for sure! He didn't believe us. But the dollar signs made him think of the easy money.

We didn't think he was actually going to do it, but as Kent and I started walking away, we realized David (John) was not with us. We both turned around at the same time and saw him standing courageously in front of the wire. Yes, he was ... Before we could even comprehend what was happening, he shouted, "It's not wor—KING!!!!" Next thing you know he was on the ground, whimpering and grasping his cajones. Not what I would consider the best way to make twenty dollars.

Moral: Don't jump to a decision. Use the *"Cool Stuff"* law of put-it-on-the-backburner: Take a break and think things through. As a rule, if something sounds too good to be true, it probably is.

MONEY TIPS

Many ways to save require no planning—just doing! Check these out:

>> Put away a dollar a day.

>> Everyday take your change and put it into a container that you cannot open. It is amazing how quickly it adds up!

>> If you can't buy it with cash, you probably can't afford it!

>> If you can't afford it, don't buy it!

>> Don't carry more money with you than you reasonably need.

>> Compare investments to find the best one.

>> Save before you spend.

>> Don't put all your eggs into one basket (more on this later).

FRIENDS & MONEY DON'T MIX

Often (not always) money and friends do not mix very well—kind of like fire and gas.

> *THE HOLY PASSION OF FRIENDSHIP IS OF SO SWEET AND STEADY AND LOYAL AND ENDURING A NATURE THAT IT WILL LAST THROUGH A WHOLE LIFETIME, IF NOT ASKED TO LEND MONEY.*
>
> —Mark Twain

Kyle: *I lent 100 bucks to a friend so he could fix his downhill mountain bike. When the day came for him to repay, he had an excuse. A week later, he had a new excuse. It took a year and a lot of hassles before I finally got my money back. It was really awkward for me to keep bringing it up, especially since I was the one doing him the favor. I forgave him, but it scarred our friendship. It*

was hard for me to trust him in other similar situations.

There are many reasons to lend money. We're not talking about a couple of bucks; we're talking about larger amounts, like a couple of hundred. Is the money worth more than the friendship, or vice versa? This is what we've learned: *If you lend someone $20 and never see that person again, it was probably worth it.*

INTERE$TING...
INTERE$TING

When you put your money into a savings account, you're lending money to the bank. For the use of your money, the bank pays you interest. Interest, then, is the return you receive for lending your money.

For example, say you invested $1,000 in a savings account at a 6% interest rate. This means you'll earn $60 of interest per year. This is called simple interest, interest paid on your principal (original investment) amount only.

COMPOUND
INTEREST

For some, compound interest is the eighth wonder of the world! Einstein called it "the greatest mathematical discovery of all time."

Compound interest is interest paid on the principal (original amount invested) AND on the accumulated interest earned. In other words, *interest on your interest*. Oh yeah, baby! It really makes your money grow.

Let's return to the above example, this time using compound interest:

Your original investment was $1,000 at 6% annual interest compounded monthly. At the end of the first month, your account would show $1,005.00. For your second month, the interest is compounded on $1,005.00 (not just $1,000). At the end of that second month, therefore, you have $1,010.02 in your account. For your third month, the interest is compounded on $1,010.02 (not just $1,005.00). Get it?

It may not seem like a lot at the beginning, but it adds up, especially on bigger investments.

Time	Simple Interest	Compound Interest
First Month	Original Investment + Interest	Original Investment + Interest = New Total
Second Month	Original Investment + Interest	New Total + Interest
Third Month	Original Investment + Interest	New Total + Interest
Each Subsequent Month	Original Investment + Interest	New Total + Interest

NOTE: The same formula applied for the length of time of your investment.

The Proof:

Let's compare: What's the difference between simple interest and compound interest for the same initial investment, over the same time period?

Simple interest at an annual rate of 6% on a $5,000 investment over 10 years will equal:

>> **$8,000.00**

Compound interest at an annual rate of 6% compounded monthly on a $5,000 investment over 10 years will equal:

>> **$8,954.24**

That's **$954.24 extra** in your pocket without lifting a finger, all thanks to compound interest. Obviously, compound interest is the way to go. When you have that option, jump on it!

THE RULE OF 72

Credit Einstein for the Rule of 72 (and for whatever financial success it brings to YOU). Simply put, the rule calculates how many years it will take for your initial investment to double using compound interest. The formula is simple:

72 / Rate of interest = Number of Years

Here's how it works: You're earning 6% interest on your investment. Divide the interest rate, 6, into 72. The answer, 12, is the number of years it will take for your investment to double at this compound interest rate. In other words, 6 x 12 = 72.

If you were earning 8%, do the math: 72 / 8 = 9 years. Use this rule to get an idea of how long it will take you to double your investment if you don't touch it.

DEPENDENCE OR INDEPENDENCE?

We hope it's not your goal to still be living with your parents at age 30. Most of us want independence but are financially dependent on others. You'll never get there by asking:

"DAD, CAN I HAVE SOME MORE MONEY SO I CAN BECOME INDEPENDENT?"

Saving and investing can truly lead you to independence. Save, invest, and become free! Don't depend on others. Once you have freedom, you have it all.

RETIREMENT

For those of us under age 20, the word "retirement" tends to freak us out. It's farther away than the moon! I doubt you're going to wake up tomorrow and suddenly be 60 years old.

But unlike the moon, you will land on retirement some day ... and it will come faster than you think. Question: What can you do to be prepared to make the latter half of your life more fun and relaxed? We don't know about you, but we would rather not be working a 9-to-5 job six days a week when we're 50. No way!

You, too, can retire early. All you have to do is start putting some money aside to invest. The sooner you start investing, the more spending money you'll have later.

Listen to this cool short story from Paul McWilliams, named by *"Smart Money"* magazine as one of the 30 most influential people in the world of investing.

A Tale of Two Brothers

Beginning in 1964, the parents of twin brothers Ben and Jerry started giving each twin $2,000 every Christmas. The parents told Ben and Jerry they would continue this tradition for ten years. This means that each brother would receive a total of $20,000.

During the first six years, Jerry found the need to spend money on various things (clothes, stereo equipment, nights on the town, etc.). During the same six years, however, Ben saw the gifts as an opportunity to get ahead and decided to invest his money every year in an S&P500 Index mutual fund (discussed in greater detail in our Wall Street chapter).

Just before Ben and Jerry received their seventh annual check, Jerry asked Ben how much he had saved. Ben said he had a total of $17,000 ($12,000 from the six checks and $5,000 in profits). Jerry basically had nothing. His clothes had worn out, and the stereo he had bought with his first check needed repair.

After hearing of his brother's success, Jerry decided to start investing as well. Determined to catch up, Jerry invested the $2,000 gift from his parents that year and the next three. Then, after the gifts stopped, he saved money from his paycheck and continued to make deposits for a total of 30 years. However, Ben, knowing he got a headstart, decided to quit making deposits when the gifts stopped and just let his account ride.

The brothers never talked about the accounts again until Jerry brought it up one day ... after 30 years of making deposits. He was certain he now had more money than Ben; after all, Ben had deposited only $20,000 — all gifts from his parents — and Jerry had deposited three times as much. Jerry didn't only save the last $8,000 given to him by his parents; he saved $52,000 from his paychecks during the 26 years that followed. This means Jerry saved a total of $60,000.

Imagine Jerry's shock when he discovered Ben still had more. As a matter of fact, Ben had 44% more money because he started six years earlier.

The moral of the story is that time makes a HUGE difference! If you start saving early, you can also decide to quit saving early. However, if you start late, you can save for the rest of your life and still end up with less money and, as a result, much less freedom to do what you want.

Note: Returns are based on the average performance of the S&P500 Index from 1926 through 1998 and include the value of reinvested dividends.

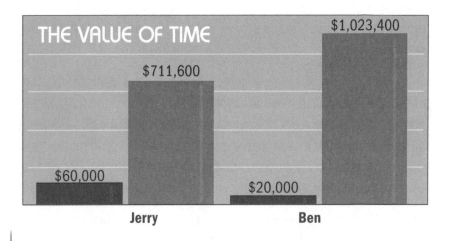

THE VALUE OF TIME

	$711,600	$1,023,400
$60,000		$20,000
Jerry		**Ben**

THE WRAP

In the end,

the more money you save,
the more frequently you save it,
the longer the length of time you save it for,
the higher return you get on your investments, and
the more diversified you are,
will determine how financially successful you will become.

Most people have an excuse not to save, even though they agree that saving is a good thing. No one is going to make you save. Take this into consideration: **Investing will make your life better.** If that's not enough to motivate you . . . what is?

Make the choice to upgrade your lifestyle! Remember what you just learned, and apply it to your life!

"Cool Stuff"

_____

_____

_____

_____

_____

_____

_____

_____

_____

_____

My "To Do" List:

☐ Pay myself first.

☐ Get my money to work for me.

☐ Make money a priority but not a god.

☐ Decide if my purchases are needs or wants.

☐ Take care of my pennies so that my dollars will take care of themselves.

☐ Look out for deals that sound "too good to be true," because they probably are.

☐ Remember opportunity cost when making spending decisions.

☐ "I must give before I get."

☐ Become familiar with fees, and don't let them take advantage of me.

☐ Be careful when mixing friends and money.

☐ Try to find investments involving compound interest.

☐ Use the Rule of 72 to help me choose the best deals.

☐ Get my freedom by investing my money wisely.

☐ Invest now! The sooner I invest, the sooner I can retire!

Check This 08 Out!

Behind the scenes of
the banking realm.

THE BANKING SYSTEM

These days it's difficult to survive using only cash. Life becomes a lot more convenient and manageable if you take advantage of the financial tools available to you ... banking tools.

Ah, the banking system! Checking accounts, savings accounts, debit cards—where would we be without 'em? Nowadays, these basics are musts for everyday purchases, to pay rent, to make mortgage payments, to register for school, and so on. They offer us not only convenient ways to pay for stuff but also profitable ways to save money. Hmmm ... We like that!

Yet we discovered that many of our friends did not really know what the financial world has to offer. You could be missing opportunities to invest and to simplify your life. Don't miss the boat!

We can hear some of you saying, "I don't have enough money to get started." Banks welcome new clients. They know that Big Clients generally start out as Small Customers. And they know that Big Clients generally stick with the financial institutions that helped them get started!

So keep reading to find out the basics of checking and savings accounts and how you can benefit!

TAKE THIS INTO ACCOUNT

Banks actually pay you to store your money. The money you earn is called "interest." The more money you have in the bank, the more interest you'll earn. In addition to paying you for holding your money, banks also offer a number of services (some free).

Why, then, would you NOT want to earn interest on your money? Why would you let it collect dust in your drawer (if you keep it that long)?

It all starts when you open an *account*, that is, you start a formal business relationship with a bank. If you don't already have a savings or a checking account, it would be wise to open one. The sooner you start using the banking system, the better.

The advantage of a checking account is that you can write checks and use debit/check/ATM cards (we'll get to that later). Savings accounts, on the other hand, offer higher interest rates but may lack flexibility.

HOW DO I SET UP
MY ACCOUNT?

Every bank has its own "terms and conditions" for savings and checking accounts. Be sure to check out the terms and conditions before you open an account.

Banks make the process of opening an account pretty simple. Be ready to supply them with what they need:

>> **Get some money!** Most banks have a minimum opening balance. It can be as low as $25 (it depends on the bank). If your account goes under the minimum, the bank usually charges a

monthly fee. (For a financial kick-start, see Make Yourself the #1 Applicant on page 91 or B.Y.O.B. on page 111.)

>> **Prove you're really who you say you are.** No, a note from your mom won't work. You'll have to show identification such as a driver's license, a passport, or a birth certificate. If you're under 18, your parents will need to be there too.

>> **Social security number.** This number is a must. It allows the government to keep track of people's earnings, retirement benefits, and much more. It is also commonly used as a personal identification number. You really should memorize it because you'll need it more and more often as you get older. (You can get an application at your local Social Security office. Check your phonebook to locate a nearby office, or check online at www.ssa.gov.)

>> **Signature.** By now, we hope you have this down. If you don't, work on one right now! The bank will use this to identify your handwriting and verify your signature whenever you make a transaction, especially on your checks. Consistency is key; it allows the bank to verify it's really you.

>> **Smile.** Bring a good mood with you. You're on your way to financial success! If that's not something to smile about, what is? Besides, people like to help someone with a smile.

BANK FEES

Keep your eye on transaction fees. Yes, banks charge fees in order to cover their expenses.

Does your bank charge a small fee every time you write a check? Every time you use your debit card? Every time you use an ATM (Automatic Teller Machine)? If you don't understand a fee, never be afraid to ASK!

Before you open an account, think about how you will be using your account. Are you going to write a large number of checks? Are you likely to do a lot of ATM transactions? Only a few? Think first so that you can determine which account is best for you.

These "little things" can really add up. Let's say your account has a $5 monthly fee and a 30-cent fee for each transaction you make. If you write two checks, swipe your debit card 15 times, and get cash at an ATM machine three times, it would cost you $11 a month and $132 a year. That's a lot of dinero!

CHECKING ACCOUNTS

At some point, you'll have to write a check. It's inevitable. You'll need to write one to pay your rent, make a car payment, pay your monthly bills, and so on. When you start looking for that first apartment, you'll be ready to move in and pay your bills with ease.

JUST BECAUSE YOU HAVE A CHECKBOOK DOES NOT MEAN YOU HAVE MONEY.

A blank check may look confusing. What are all those blank lines and odd numbers? In less than a minute, you'll understand this simple process.

Read the following descriptions for each of the numbered sections in this check. Note that some items are preprinted on the check and some you write:

* Keep in mind this is a sample. Not every check is the same.

>> **1.** Name of the bank.

>> **2.** Date that you wrote the check.

>> **3.** Check number. This makes it easy for you to identify and record the checks you've written. It also makes the bank's processing easier.

>> **4.** "Pay to the Order of." On this line, you write the person's name or company's name you wish to pay.

>> **5.** Name of the person who owns the checking account from which the money will be withdrawn.

>> **6.** This is your personal note space, so that you can remind yourself why you wrote this particular check.

>> **7.** Check routing number. This number identifies your bank to other banks. When another bank receives this check, it will use this number to identify your bank and process this check.

FACT: All the digits at the bottom of the check are called MICR codes (Magnetic Image Character Recognition codes). The ink used in printing these numbers contains iron so that scanners can read them magnetically. The reason some of these numbers are shaped funny is because each digit must be a certain size to include enough iron-ink for the scanners to read accurately.

>> **8.** Check number (in MICR format). Note: This is the same number in step 3.

>> **9.** Your bank account number. Your bank will scan this number to process your transaction and charge the total to your account.

>> **10.** The amount to be paid. You'll write this amount out in full using both words and numbers. The "squiggle" at the end of the line is for safety. It prevents anyone from changing the amount you wrote on the check.

>> **11.** The signature of the owner of the checking account gives permission to transfer the money.

>> **12.** In this space, the transaction amount will be MICR-printed on the check when it is processed so it can be scanned with all the other necessary information.

>> **13.** The same transaction amount in 10 above, written in numerical form.

THE BALANCING ACT

Writing the check? That's the easy part. Balancing your account—that's where most people drop the ball!

You must balance your checkbook to keep track of your money. This is really important because it shows you:

>> If your checks have cleared.
>> If your deposits were entered.
>> What you're paying in fees.
>> What your balance is (as of the statement date).

"How do I actually do this?"

The place to balance your checkbook is on the back of each bank statement. You will find step-by-step instructions that guide you through the process.

Make sure each transaction in your checkbook matches your bank statement. If you don't keep records of this, you could end up spending a lot of your time, effort, and money trying to figure it out and fix it all later.

Remember: You need to enter in your checkbook each check you write and deposit you make. If you don't do this, you will have no idea how much money you have in your account!

Kyle: *When I signed up for my first credit card, I specified that the total monthly balance on my card be automatically deducted from my bank account on the due date. When I went in to pick up my surfboard after waiting five long weeks, my credit card was rejected. Because it wasn't accepted, I couldn't pay for my surfboard. AND I COULDN'T GO SURFING! A real problem! Worse, I had to come home and go through several months of bank and credit card statements to see what went wrong.*

Problem: If I had gone through my earlier bank and credit card statements, that never would have happened. I would have discovered the problem months before! Instead, when I received my bank statements, I glanced at them quickly and overlooked the totals. Bad move!

As it turned out, the bank had set up my account so that the minimum payment was being deducted every month instead of the full balance due. My card was slightly over my credit limit, and I was being charged interest on the unpaid balance. I went in to the bank, and they helped me correct it all.

My lesson: Save a lot of time, effort, and money by balancing my bank statements regularly.

A+++++++++++! !!!!!!!!!!!

"**M**y checkbook balance doesn't agree with my bank statement balance!"

Calm down and take a breather . . . it's going to be all right. The problem might be that:

>> You have forgotten to subtract a check or ATM withdrawal.
>> You have forgotten to subtract some of your bank fees.
>> The bank has not received a deposit you sent in.
>> You have recorded the wrong amount when you wrote a check or deposit.
>> A check hasn't cleared yet.

Tip 1: Set up online access with your bank so that you can check your up-to-date statement and balance. No more anxiety attack waiting for your monthly statement to arrive in the mail.

Tip 2: Balance your checkbook as soon as you can! Your bank may have a time limit for reporting and correcting an error. It helps to be consistent. Balance it as soon as you get your statement; then you don't need to think or worry about doing it later.

Tip 3: Keep your debit and credit receipts to compare the charges on your bank statement with your credit card statements. (Good idea to keep receipts because you will sometimes need to return products.)

Tip 4: Not all banks return cancelled (that is, cashed) checks to you. If your bank does mail them to you, hold on to them. Keep them in a safe place for about five years. Your cancelled checks are your receipts. Who knows? You may have to prove a payment was made to someone, even years later! Store the checks in a large envelope or box; write the date range on the outside; and then file the envelope or box in a safe place. Easy ... and definitely the smart thing to do.

DEBIT CARDS

Also known as check and ATM cards, debit cards look like credit cards, but they work like cash or personal checks.

When you use a debit card, money is deducted directly from your checking account. Debit means "to subtract." Debit cards only allow you to withdraw money that is in your account. Because the money you're using is yours, you are not borrowing from MasterCard, Visa, or any other company. The funds are taken immediately from your account.

In other words, a debit card is a "pay now" way to buy, whereas a credit card is "pay later." Clearly, everyone must learn to control spending. Debit cards do not stop us from spending; but they do stop us from borrowing. You can still go broke, so use it wisely.

2K TIP

PACK IT. Save your dinero! Eating out hits the wallet hard. When possible, bring some food and drink from home, and save the extra cash for the things you have to pay for, like gas or more "Cool Stuff" books.

YOUR PIN NUMBER

Question: If you lose your debit card, what prevents someone from using it? Answer: Your PIN number.

A debit card requires a PIN number (personal identification number). PINs are usually four digits, and you can use any combination you want. Your PIN number is your security. Keep it secret!

When you use your debit card, merchants will require you either to enter your PIN in their card machine or to sign a copy of the receipt.

"How do I get a debit card?"

Talk to your bank. Of course, you'll need to have a checking or savings account first. In most cases, you must be 18.

"What else must I know about debit cards?"

>> If you are under 18, you must have a guardian share responsibility for the account.
>> Understandably, it is usually easier to get a debit card

than a credit card.

>> Debit cards work like superfast checks—each purchase amount is subtracted from your bank account ... only faster!

>> Merchants prefer debit cards over checks, because debit cards don't bounce—that is, they do not allow you to write a check for more money than you have in your bank account.

>> The debit card has no grace period.

>> If you return goods you purchased with a debit card, the transaction is treated the same way as if you had paid with cash or check, meaning the refund amount will go right back into your account.

>> You may have to pay transaction fees each time you use the debit card.

"What if my debit card is lost or stolen?"

Do not pass Go! Report it to the bank (your carrier) immediately! The sooner you report the loss, the more protection you will have.

Of course, check your account statements carefully. If you find an unauthorized charge, call the toll-free fraud claim number to report such purchases and withdrawals.

Tips for Using Debit Cards

>> Report a lost or stolen card ASAP.

>> Memorize your PIN number. This is a must!

>> Don't use an obvious PIN number, one that a thief may easily guess or discover, like your birthday or your address. (If a thief gets your wallet or purse, he has that information!)

>> Never give your PIN to anybody.

>> Always keep tabs on how much is available in your account so you will notice if money is mysteriously disappearing (if, for example, somebody knows your PIN).

>> Keep your receipts in a safe place. A thief could easily get

your name and card number from them and order goods through catalogues or via telephone. Your card doesn't need to be missing in order for it to be misused.

SAVINGS ACCOUNTS
AND CDs

To understand "savings bank essentials," let's look at Mr. and Mrs. Smith. The Smiths have several accounts:

1 The Smiths deposit $200 every month into their savings account with First Bank. In return, First Bank pays the Smiths interest on the money in their account.

2 A few years ago, the Smiths bought a home. To buy that home, they borrowed $100,000 (a mortgage) from First Bank. In return, the Smiths pay back First Bank part of that $100,000 plus interest every month.

As you see, (1) savings banks pay interest to depositors in return for holding depositors' money, and (2) savings banks receive interest by lending depositors' money to others (for example, for car loans and home mortgages).

Of course, banks lend money at a higher interest rate than they pay to you for holding your money. The difference is the bank's profit.

Bank investments are generally considered "safe" because banks run few risks. Savings banks are famous for their classic "passbook account," a simple account that pays you interest on your balance. Savings banks also offer certificates of deposit, which are discussed next.

CERTIFICATES OF DEPOSIT (CDs)

Nah, you won't be able to listen to these CDs! In the world of banking, CD stands for "certificate of deposit." When you put your money into a "bank CD," you promise to leave the money untouched for a specific period of time (say, 3 months or 12 months or longer). The bank gives you a certificate, basically a valuable receipt!

At the end of the time period, you turn in your certificate and receive the full amount you put in plus the interest your money has earned. Sweet!

Now, you're wondering, "How does it differ from a savings account?" Glad you asked! Here's the difference: CD interest rates are higher than savings account rates because you agree not to touch your money for a specific period of time. The longer the term, the higher the interest rate.

Now here's some fancy banking lingo for you: "date of maturity." That's when the CD term (length of time invested) is over. Now you can cash it in. As we said earlier, you get all your investment back AND all the interest you've earned.

Tip: If you find it hard to hold onto your money, a CD might be right for you. Why? Because once you make the investment, you can't touch it ... unless you're willing to pay the early withdrawal penalty. No way!

"Which CD is best for me?"

The interest rates that banks offer for CDs is usually

determined by the period of time you "lock up" your money in the CD and by the total amount of the investment. Banks pay slightly higher interest rates on their CDs than they pay for their savings or checking accounts.

A PAPER A DAY... Read the newspaper, watch the news, or check the headline news on the Internet at least ten minutes a day. Even if you're busy, just skim it. Knowing a little about a lot of things makes you a more interesting person.

As you consider the term of the investment, think carefully: How likely is it that you will need the money during that term?

THE WRAP

So there you have it . . . Basic Banking 101: enough to get you started, to make you comfortable with the banking system, and to start you thinking of how you can take advantage of what it offers.

Always be on the lookout for new information, tips, and methods that could save you time and money.

My "To Do" List:

❏ Set up a bank account (if you don't already have one).
❏ Consider getting a debit card.
❏ Always keep my eyes on the fees.
❏ Make sure I know how to fill out a check and balance my checkbook.
❏ Consider investing in a CD.

What's Wall Street? 09

Invest for a
brighter future.

THE STOCK MARKET

For most of us, the stock market is some different universe where old people hang out and talk about stuff we know nothing about. We've all heard of it, but what is it? The stock market offers excellent investment opportunities, but why do some people make millions while others end up broke?

A (VERY) BRIEF HISTORY:

Wall Street got its name from the wall that Dutch settlers built to protect themselves from Native Americans and pirates in the 17th century. A path was created next to the wall, and after the path grew larger, it was eventually named "Wall Street." There, under a buttonwood tree, on May 17, 1792, people started trading stocks.

At first, only "members" could trade stocks. As more information became available, more and more people began to invest in this "stock market." Trading gradually moved from under the tree to several small buildings, eventually growing into the financial center it is today—in New York City.

WHAT'S A "STOCK"?

A "stock" is a certificate of ownership in a company. When you own a share of stock, you own a piece of the business—sweeeeet! You are a "shareholder." Today, there are over 10,000 publicly traded companies available to choose from and invest in.

> **"Cool Stuff"**
>
> IF YOUR FAVORITE COMPANY IS PUBLICLY TRADED, THEN YOU CAN BECOME PART OWNER BY BUYING ITS STOCK!

SHOW ME THE MONEY!

This is the part everyone loves ... making the dough. But you can also lose money. No one can predict what will happen to a stock. How much money you make depends on how well the company does.

The two main ways to make money in the stock market are:

Dividends: Certain companies pay their shareholders dividends. If the company does well, its board of directors may decide to share a portion of its profits with shareholders in the form of a "dividend." There's no guarantee, of course, that the board will decide to issue dividends—and if so, how much.

Capital Gain: If you sell your shares at a profit, the money you make is called a *capital gain*. The gain is the difference between your original invested amount and the amount you sold the stock for.

RISK AND REWARD

Many people call the stock market a "crap shoot," meaning it's a gamble ... too much luck and not enough strategy. True, a stock can go down in value. No one knows what will happen! But the good news is that you can choose the level of risk you're willing to take.

Low-risk stocks include "blue-chip" stocks, that is, stocks in solid, well-established, generally conservative companies. The theory is that well-established companies are less likely to lose their worth.

High-risk investments include startup companies. Obviously, new, unfamiliar companies run greater risks of failure.

Zero-risk ... actually ... we just made this up. There's no such thing as an investment that involves no risk (even out of the stock market).

INVESTING ISN'T ABOUT GUARANTEES. IT'S ABOUT BALANCING RISK WITH REASONABLE EXPECTATIONS OF REWARD.

—*The Wall Street Journal Guide to Understanding Personal Finance*

Risk is everywhere when it comes to investing. Every investor must decide what level of risk he or she is comfortable with. In general, there are three types of people.

Conservatives don't like to take risks. They always play it safe.

Moderates like to "mix it up" by taking some risks but backing themselves up with low-risk investments too.

Speculators like to take big chances that might bring large rewards.

As a rule, the safer the investment, the smaller the return. Another way of saying it: The greater the risk, the more you

2K TIP

SOCIAL STATUS. Don't do something simply to change what other people think of you. Be more concerned about your character than your reputation. Your character is who you really are, and your reputation is just what other people think of you.

can make (or lose). The choice is up to you. If you avoid risk and take no chances, you risk missing out. You can't expect huge earnings from low-risk investments like certificates of deposit (CDs), notes, bank accounts, and blue chip stocks.

DIVERSIFY
OR ELSE

Risk will always be there. What's the best way to protect yourself from risk? Diversify your investments. "Don't put all your eggs in one basket!" This means you should invest in a variety of options. If you take the expression literally, you'll find that all it takes is one accident for the basket of eggs to fall and break—where you'd lose everything in it.

Diversification options include:

>> Several different stocks
(instead of only one)

>> CDs

>> Notes

>> Bonds

>> Treasury Bills
(called "T Bills")

>> Mutual funds (groups of "equities" managed by experts)

>> Commodities (like gold, silver, platinum, diamonds, grain, oil, etc.)

ALLOCATION

This can sound complicated. It's really not. Asset allocation is just a fancy way of describing how you divide your portfolio (see "What's That Mean?" on page 187 for a definition). One example of asset allocation: 50% of your total investment in stocks, 35% in CDs and bonds, and 15% in cash.

Obviously, this 50/35/15 split is not "best" for everyone. It depends on your investing objectives at the time. You will certainly change your split throughout your life.

If you think "danger" is your middle name, you might want to buy the riskier stocks now, while you're younger. If you lose, you can earn back the money without worrying about missing your mortgage payments. When you get older and are supporting a family, such risky investments might not be comfortable. If they fail, you can really leave your family out in the cold!

THE "UNREAL" VALUE

If your stock goes up, you own something more valuable—but you don't actually see the money until you sell your shares. (Unless you're receiving some payments in dividends, like we talked about earlier). That was a huge mistake a lot of people made in the 2001 stock market crash.

The Technology market skyrocketed. It seemed everyone was getting rich overnight. However, these people were really only rich on paper. Their stocks went up, and theoretically they had a lot of money. Some began spending and bought fancy cars and huge houses. The problem was, they never sold their stock. They thought their stocks would keep going up and/or the dividends would keep rolling in. But they didn't.

Then the market crashed (that is, the value of stocks declined). The people who didn't sell their stock faced massive financial problems. They had spent huge amounts of money that they never actually had. A lot of "paper millionaires" almost went bankrupt overnight. It wasn't too pretty.

A long time ago, John D. Rockefeller, a billionaire stock market genius, was asked why he was so successful. He replied, "I always sold too early."

It is okay to hold onto your stock if you predict it will go up or if it's a long-term investment, but remember what goes up can also come down. Values can drop at any time. And when companies aren't making money, dividends aren't paid. So beware.

MEASURING PERFORMANCE

Performance: Measurement of the overall well-being of a stock or the stock market.

When most people think of measuring the stock market, the first thing that might come to mind is the "Dow Jones Industrial Average," but there are many other benchmarks (or indexes) to check how certain areas of the stock market are performing.

What's an "index"? It's a collection of stocks measured as a group to indicate the stock market's overall performance. Without indexes, you'd have to analyze thousands of stocks in magazines, newspapers, and the Internet to get the overall feel of the market.

Here are some popular indexes:

>> Dow Jones: Tracks 30 large industrial blue chip stocks and is widely known for its very popular index, the "Dow Jones Industrial Average"

>> NASDAQ: Lists tech stocks. (See page 189 for a definition.)

>> Wilshire 5000 Equity Index: Measures all the stocks traded on NASDAQ and on the New York and the American Stock Exchanges

>> Standard & Poor's 500: Reports on the stocks of 500 well-known large companies

>> Russell 2000: Tracks small-company stocks

Tip: If you're after one particular stock, you can find the daily high and low in most newspapers, the news, etc. Or you can check the Internet for constantly updated stock data, graphs, and tips.

Warren Buffet once said, "It's time in the market, not timing the market" that will give you the greatest profits when investing in the stock market.

It's easy to get spooked and sell your shares when your stock drops in value, but you must expect the market to fluctuate. We have been told that one of the greatest dangers is not sticking with your stocks. Generally, you're more likely to lose money if you sell in a downturn instead of riding it out and thinking long-term.

Unless you plan to be a day trader (someone who constantly watches specific stocks and sells shares daily—not recommended), you might want to leave your portfolio alone and consider it a long-term investment. Holding your stocks through the ups and the downs is referred to as the "buy and hold strategy." Most of the time, when you buy and sell stocks less often, you'll outperform those who trade frequently. This may not always be the case, but it's a good rule to follow.

WHAT DETERMINES THE PRICE OF A STOCK?

Who determines the price for each stock? Well, actually the investors do. A stock is worth only what someone is willing to pay for it. There is no set value. If buyers think a publicly traded company has a lot of potential, the stock goes up in value because people want to buy it. In most cases, if the demand is high, the value will be too. On the other hand, if a company is managed poorly and begins to lose money, investors won't want to buy its stock, which causes the price to go down.

WHAT'S THAT MEAN?

If you make an effort to learn some of the most common stock market and investment terms, you'll be waaaaay ahead of most people (maybe even your parents). Since people only hear what they understand, it's worth the effort!

OK, I'LL GET YOUR DINNER SPOT

BLAH, BLAH BLAH BLAH BLAH SPOT

Don't be the household pet of the conversation!

Mutual fund: A mutual fund is a variety of investments under the guidance of a fund manager or a group of managers. Some mutual funds include bonds, CDs, minerals, and real estate as well as stocks. Mutual funds provide opportunity for every investor, even an individual with little money (for example $200), to invest in a diversified way. This is a good example of not putting all your eggs in one basket.

Bull market, bear market: Stock enthusiasts love to use these terms: "Looks like a bull market, Bob." A bull market describes a period of time where values rise—a good thing. A bear market, on the other hand, describes a period when stock values fall at least 15%—not so good.

And now, at no extra charge, here is an interesting explanation of these terms. In ancient Rome, bulls and bears were forced to fight in the Coliseum for entertainment. The bulls would buck upwards (symbolizing a market on the rise), and the bears would try to pull downwards (representing a falling market).

Bond, James Bond. No, just kidding. A stock represents ownership in a company. A bond, on the other hand, represents a loan (usually over $1,000) that pays interest. Basically, you agree to lend a certain amount of money to a corporation or a government body for a set period of time. Over this period, the company pays you a set interest rate on your money. You can buy and sell bonds; their value rises and falls, depending on interest rates and the bond market.

Portfolio: A collection of all your investments—all your CDs, individual stocks and bonds, mutual funds—the works!

Blue-chip describes the stocks of larger, well-established, well-known companies such as IBM, AT&T, GE, etc. The name comes from the blue chip in poker, the chip that has the highest value. Note: Blue-chip stocks offer no more guarantees than any other stock.

Dow Jones Industrial Average is a specific formula that calculates the average value of 30 U.S. blue-chip stocks of industrial companies (excluding transportation and utility companies). The average shows the general health of the stock prices as a whole. Charles Dow created the DJIA in 1896.

NYSE (New York Stock Exchange): This is one of the organized stock markets in New York. It is the oldest and largest stock exchange in the U.S.

NASDAQ (National Association of Securities Dealers Automated Quotations, pronounced "NAZ-dak") is a stock exchange where the trade orders take place only through a computer network; there is no stock-trading floor as on the New York Stock Exchange. Many high technology companies are listed on the NASDAQ.

AMEX (short for the American Stock Exchange) is another major stock market, located in New York.

A **CEO** (Chief Executive Officer) is usually the head of an organization and can also be the company's president. The CEO is principally responsible for the activities of a company.

WHAT'S THAT SMELL? If someone offers you a breath mint, always say "Yes." They may have information you can't smell.

The **CFO** (Chief Financial Officer) is responsible for handling funds, signing checks, keeping financial records, and the financial planning for a corporation. The CFO may also have the additional title of treasurer, controller, or vice president of finance.

The **CIO** (Chief Information Officer) is responsible for all aspects of a company's information technology and systems.

The **COO** (Chief Operating Officer) is usually the president or executive vice president and is responsible for the day-to-day management of the company's operations. The COO reports to the CEO.

A **stockbroker** buys and sells stocks for his or her clients. Stockbrokers are usually paid a commission (a percentage of the trade) or a flat fee per trade. There are two main types:

#1 A **full-service stockbroker (advisory)** may do research for clients, make stock recommendations, give advice, take care of transactions, and help with other aspects of your investment portfolio.

#2 A **discount stockbroker (non-advisory broker)** buys and sells on your demand. Discount stockbrokers usually don't provide research or make recommendations. As a result, their cost is usually lower.

Stock split: When a company believes its stock price is too high to attract new investors, it may split its stock, that is, literally divide it. Let's say you own 100 shares currently valued at $60 a share. The company decides the price is too high so it splits "two for one." You now own 200 shares valued at $30 each! Stocks can also be split three for one, three for two, and other ways.

Reverse split reduces your current number of shares. For example, 1 for every 2 you own. Of course, in a reverse split, the value of each share rises. Companies do a reverse split to hike their low stock prices and increase the range of buyers to investors who normally do not buy low-price stocks (for example, stocks valued under $5).

Procrastination: We'll get to that later. ☺

Capital gain is the profit you make when you sell an investment for more than you bought it. For example, if you bought a stock for $100 and you sold it for $150, your capital gain is $50.

DRIPs (Dividend Reinvestment Plans) are usually bought directly through the company you have invested in or from a transfer agent. As the name suggests, DRIPs directly reinvest your dividends back into the company, which is good because you save the cost of broker's fees.

"HOW DO I READ STOCK QUOTES?"

Of course stock quotes are confusing ... that is, until you know what all the abbreviations and numbers stand for. Then they're a snap!

Let's look at a make-believe stock quote for Corporation X (CRPX):

Stock	Market/Exchange	Open	Low	High	Close/Last
CRPX	NYSE	50.50	49.80	51.50	51

Net Chg.	P/E	Yld (%)	Div	Vol.(100s)	High-52 week	Low-52 week
+1	40	3.0	1.50	274	70.25	45.35

Now let's look at what each of the column headings means:

>> Stock: Also known as the Listing, Ticker, or Symbol, this is the abbreviation of the company's name as it appears on the stock exchange: CRPX.

>> Market/Exchange: Identifies the market or stock exchange where this particular stock is traded. CRPX is traded on the NYSE. Other stocks might show NASDAQ, AMEX, etc.

>> Open: The price of the stock at the moment it opened for trade that day.

>> Low: The lowest value the stock was traded for that day.

>> High: The highest value the stock was traded for that day.

>> Close/Last: The value of the stock at closing time that day.

>> Net Chg.: The Net Change, or the difference between the closing price on the day before and the closing price on the current day.

>> P/E: The Price to Earnings ratio gives investors a feel for the value of the stock. Is it "cheap," or is it "expensive"? How much are you paying (P) for the company's earnings (E)? The ratio is useful in comparing the value of one stock to another.

>> Yld: The yield, the percentage of dividends that the company's stock pays out compared to its price or value. CRPX's yield of 3.0 means that if you invested $1000 in CRPX, then you would get about

$30 (a yield of 3%) in dividends that year.

>> Div: The dividend, the amount of earnings the investor will receive per share from the company.

>> Vol.: The volume shows the number of shares traded that day for CRPX. Multiply that number by 100 (see the "100s" in parentheses?) to find the actual total.

>> High/Low - 52 week: Sometimes referred to as the "Yr high" or "Yr low," this shows the highest and lowest prices paid for a share of CRPX during the previous year.

THE WRAP

The stock market isn't such a dangerous place if you know the tricks of the trade. It can be a very good place to invest. We're not financial analysts, but we know that knowledge is the key. The more knowledge you have, the better chance you have of making money. Always do your homework, look for more information, and learn new techniques to invest for a brighter future!

Check out these sites for more information:

>> www.teenanalyst.com
>> www.younginvestor.com
>> www.fool.com/teens
>> www.teenvestor.com
>> www.investsmart.coe.uga.edu
>> www.beginnersinvest.about.com
>> www.amatuerinvestor.org

My "To Do" List:

❏ Realize that there are two main ways to make money from stocks: dividends or capital gain.

❏ Accept the fact that investing has no guarantees. Risk will always be there.

❏ Understand that the greater the risk I take, the more I stand to make or lose.

❏ Diversify my investments! Don't put all my eggs in one basket.

❏ Allocate my assets by balancing my portfolio with different types of investments.

❏ Avoid following the hype or trends in the market.

❏ Consider using the buy and hold strategy, and think long-term. Don't expect too much too soon.

❏ Recognize that there are many ways to measure the stock market's performance.

❏ Realize that the market has short-term fluctuations. Don't let them discourage me and steer me away from my long-term plans.

❏ Understand the lingo of the market and how to read stock quotes.

Buying With Plastic 10

Are credit cards
friends ...
or foes?

FRIEND
OR FOE?

Who would have thought such a small piece of plastic could give you so much freedom and convenience—and at the same time have the potential to make your life a nightmare? Some say credit cards are great; others say they are "evil money-sucking demons." In the end, it comes down to how you handle your money. It's not the card ... it's YOU. Are you conservative in your spending, or do you throw your money at store clerks?

No doubt about it: Credit cards are convenient. It's a means of identification. It allows you to order products on the Internet or by phone, and it can be a lifesaver when you suddenly remember to buy your mom's birthday present half an hour before the mall closes. Yup ... very convenient!

SO WHAT'S THE FUSS
ABOUT CREDIT CARDS?

With the right credit card, a new surfboard, powerful stereo system, and cool wardrobe are all at your fingertips. Buy now, pay later. But (you knew there was a "but" coming) that's where people get into trouble—BIG trouble. Here's the deal:

WHEN YOU USE A CREDIT CARD, YOU ARE NOT USING YOUR MONEY; YOU ARE BORROWING MONEY!

Of course, you have to pay it back. In return for borrowing money, the company charges the user a fee, a finance charge. Depending on how long you take to repay, your purchase could cost you more than you ever dreamed.

THINK BEFORE
YOU SWIPE

A lot of people are afraid of credit cards, and they have every right to be, especially if they are impulse buyers. That rectangular slice of plastic can get you into a serious financial mess. Controlling your spending is a must!

Answer these two questions: One, "Is this a need, or is it a want?" Two, "Would I make the same purchase if I were paying cash?"

Our friend Amanda loved credit cards (for about the first year) and shopping sprees. A dangerous combination! When the bill came,

"Cool Stuff"

IT'S EASY TO FALL INTO DEBT, BUT YOU HAVE TO DIG YOUR WAY OUT.

she

always paid the minimum amount. Once a card reached its limit, she'd apply for another one. Who could blame her for bragging about all her new dresses and shoes? After all, most still had price tags on them! Her system worked, as we said ... for about a year.

At the end of her one-year spree, Amanda was drowning in debt ... $9,000, to be exact. Yes, she was paying the minimum amounts, but that meant 18% interest! And the ridiculously high interest meant her debt was still growing.

Now her credit card bills are so high that she struggles to make her monthly payments. Worse, most of her payments only cover interest due. Very little goes toward reducing her actual debt. She has no spending money, no car, and no freedom. Her bad decisions, unnecessary purchases, minimum payments, and multiple cards have made her life a nightmare.

Amanda isn't alone. Credit cards have hurt many, many people. But not without their permission—or their bad spending habits! An administrator at the University of Indiana said, "We lose more students to credit card debt than to academic failure." Yikes!

Tip: Use the Stop, Drop, and Roll technique if you're having trouble controlling your purchases:

Stop: Ask yourself, "Do I really need this?"
Drop: Drop the goods—NOW!
Roll: Roll out of there as quickly as you can.

Note: This method works not only with credit cards but also with cash purchases. A slightly different version of this method also works when your clothes are on fire.

BEFORE YOU GET A CARD

Learn all you can about credit cards before you get your first one. And if you already have one, it's even more important for you to learn about 'em! Either way, read on ... Who knows, by the end of this chapter, you might be able to help out your friends and even your parents.

Always shop around. Search, compare, and find out what's available. Like buying a car, you should never get the first credit card you can or sign up impulsively. If you do, you are not a good candidate to own a card in the first place.

All credit cards are not created equal; some cost more than others. Some might throw in additional benefits like frequent-flyer miles and cool gifts. Check around for a card that really helps you.

Three main things to research are:

>> Finance charges: Every bank and every card company charges you interest for money you borrowed. Interest rates vary, but they are always measured as a percentage, and it can be *18% or more each year.* Do the math ... Ouch!

>> **Annual fee:** Most credit card companies charge a flat annual fee (whether you use the card or not). The actual amount will vary from company to company. With your research, you should be able to find a card with no yearly fee.

>> **Grace period or free period:** This is a specific period of time between when you're billed and when you have to make a payment. Some creditors may not offer a grace period at all, but most do, so try to find the longest one possible. Always try to pay in full and on time. If an emergency comes up and you can't pay your bill, the grace period can save you money. Interest will be deferred during the grace period. At the end of this period, you will start being charged interest—so watch out!

"Cool Stuff"

PAYING IN FULL AND ON TIME EVERY MONTH WILL ALWAYS OUTWEIGH EVEN THE LOWEST INTEREST RATE, BECAUSE YOU WILL THEN PAY NO INTEREST AT ALL.

THE FINE PRINT

Always read the fine print so that you know exactly what you're committing to before signing on the dotted line. For example, be sure to check out the following:

Transaction fees: Some cards charge users a small fee every time they use their cards. You can bet these little fees really add up!

Cash advance: A cash advance is when you withdraw cash instead of making a purchase. How much cash you can pull out depends on your credit card agreement, your limit, and your card's current balance. The credit card company may charge a fee for a cash advance, or it may charge you a higher rate of interest on a cash advance than it charges on purchases. But beware: Most credit cards don't permit a grace period for cash advances, even if they do permit a grace period for credit purchases. The issuer can charge you interest from the day you withdraw the money.

Exceeding your credit limit: Every card has an agreed-on limit, the maximum amount of money you can borrow. Your credit limit is determined by a variety of factors, such as your credit history, your annual income, your outstanding debts, and your ability to pay.

Late payment: If you don't pay the minimum amount by the due date, you might have to pay a late fee ($25 or more).

Monthly fee: Some creditors charge a monthly fee whether you use the card or not. Obviously not the way to go!

WARNING: DON'T PAY UP-FRONT FEES!

Most legitimate issuers do not require up-front fees (unless it's a secured card). As a general rule, you should not need to pay to get a credit card. If you have good credit, you should be able to get one. If you have bad credit, no legitimate company is likely to give you a card anyway. In either case, watch out for up-front fees.

"WHAT'S THAT MEAN?"

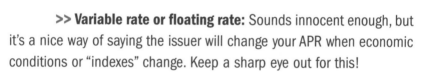

Glad you asked! The terms below are "musts." You'll be waaaay ahead when you know them!

>> **Issuer:** The bank or financial institution issuing the card. They create the terms and conditions you must agree with if you want to use the card.

>> **APR (Annual Percentage Rate):** The yearly interest you're paying to use the card (that is, borrow money), always expressed as a percent. You'll want the lowest percentage you can find.

>> **Variable rate or floating rate:** Sounds innocent enough, but it's a nice way of saying the issuer will change your APR when economic conditions or "indexes" change. Keep a sharp eye out for this!

>> **"Pre-Approved!"** Me? Aw, shucks. Sounds as if you're guaranteed to receive the card, right? WRONG! It simply means that you were chosen to receive the offer because you met some basic criteria of creditworthiness. In other words, "pre-approved" is meaningless ... just an attempt to impress you.

>> **Loyalty scheme points:** For each dollar you spend using the credit card, you'll earn a certain number of points that you can convert into discounts and free vouchers for useful things such as gasoline, airfare points, and groceries. Yes! A bonus.

Note: Refer back to this section whenever you want! (It's not cheating.)

"WHAT'S A SECURED CREDIT CARD?"

Tom is a credit risk. No bank will give him a credit card, but they know that their risk is minimal IF a card is linked to Tom's bank account (or if Tom deposits security money to back up his card). Either way, if Tom fails to pay his monthly bill, the bank deducts the payment straight from this account. No risk at all!

To get a *secured card*, you have to deposit an amount of money into the bank account that will be equal to the limit on your card. These cards are a great option if you want to build credit history or are not quite ready for the responsibilities that come with a standard credit card.

APPLYING FOR A CREDIT CARD

Before applying for a credit card you should make sure you:

>> Can resist the urge to overspend.
>> Know that using a credit card is a form of borrowing.
>> Know the terms of the contract you are committing to!
>> Know you can make your payments in full each month.
(If you can't repay in full each month, then the balance due becomes a really high-interest loan, and you should not have a credit card.)

Kent: *If you want a specific card from a certain credit company, make a few phone calls to find out how. I wanted credit* *points for flying miles, so I called United Airlines and asked how to get a United Mileage Plus Visa. They told me, and I applied. (At that time, I had no previous credit history, so I was turned down. Hey, at least I tried.)*

If I'm rejected, should I just reapply?

Reapplying again and again can lower your credit rating and make it harder to get a card the next time you apply to that company (or even to other companies, for that matter). Instead of reapplying, go for a credit card with a smaller company (department store, gas station, etc.) and work at building a good credit history (more on this point later). You have a better chance of getting the cards you want when you have a solid credit history.

After being refused by the major credit card companies like Visa and MasterCard, one of our friends applied for a card at her local department store, and she was accepted. She made her payments regularly and established a good solid credit history. Later, she applied for a Visa card. With her excellent payment record, she was approved!

CHECKIN' YOUR BILL

How can you find an error on your bill if you don't even look at it? Be sure to check for mistakes! Your bill can tell you a lot. It shows what you owed at the start of your statement period, what you owe now, and every payment and purchase made in between.

To begin, learn your rights. When you receive a credit card, you also receive a statement outlining the billing rules. What are your rights? Know them, so that if you find a mistake on your bill, you can question the charge. "What? $50 for a candy bar! $500 for exotic underwear I never bought! No way!"

Of course, you can decide to debate these charges and:

>> 1. Write to your creditor. Find the address for billing inquiries on your statement. Be sure to include your name, address, account number, and details concerning the error (date, amount charged, etc.).

>> 2. Send your letter right away! Sometimes the debating process can take a while. Most credit card agencies have a cut-off date by which you can submit your inquiry. Get the letter to them before this date; otherwise, you are stuck paying for that exotic underwear you never bought ... unless, of course, you *did* buy them.

Result: The creditor must acknowledge your complaint in writing within 30 days (unless your billing inquiry states otherwise or the problem has been resolved).

CREDIT CARD PAYMENTS

"Cool Stuff"

IF YOU CAN'T AFFORD TO PAY OFF
YOUR BILL IN FULL EACH MONTH, THEN
YOU'RE SPENDING TOO MUCH.

When it comes time to pay your bill, the best thing you can do is completely ignore the numbers beside the "minimum payment" line and skip straight to the "balance" line. If you only pay the minimum amount, you'll end up handing over a lot of extra money to the credit card company. Yep, that's right, your old buddy "interest."

If you pay the balance in full, you won't waste any money on interest, and you'll have more to spend on real stuff (like a car to go with the expensive gloves you just bought). So, do more than just look at the balance, and always try to pay it in full. Here's a shocking fact:

Half of all college students with credit cards do not pay their balances in full every month.

"AAAHHHHH! MY CARD HAS BEEN STOLEN!"

Whether it has been stolen, lost, or ingested (ok, actually if it has been lost or stolen), call the card issuer immediately. If you ingested it, it's the hospital's problem, but that too will pass (no pun intended). Most companies have a 24-hour toll-free love line service—oops, scratch that, 24-hour toll-free consumer help line—for reporting and canceling missing cards. This number will usually be on the back of your billing statement.

Once you report the card stolen, your liability is usually limited. That means if the thief has taken your card on a shopping spree and put a deposit on a new Ferrari, you don't have to pay the whole $20,000. Usually it's limited to something between $50 and $250, but it varies among credit card companies. Note: You don't get to keep the Ferrari, either.

Tip: If you'd lose your head if it weren't screwed on, you may have a hard time getting or even keeping your card. If you're prone to losing your card, credit card companies can refuse to give you another one. So, try to hold on to them!

"WHAT'S MY LIMIT?"

When it comes to your credit limit, remember that more isn't always better. Sure it can be nice to have a huge limit on your card, but unless you need it, it can cause more problems than it's worth.

First, it's easier to spend too much if you have too much. Second, lenders can view a huge credit limit as a liability because it gives you the opportunity to place yourself in greater debt.

YOUR CREDIT SCORE, RATING, AND HISTORY

When creditors see "you," what they really see is your credit rating, your credit score, and your credit history. All are very important! These factors will affect how lenders treat you and whether they grant you credit. If they decide to grant you credit, this information helps determine how much credit you're worthy of getting and at what rate.

Always work at maintaining a good credit score, rating, and history. As we said earlier, the best way to do this is to always pay your balance in full and on time. Don't screw up here!

Your Score: Yes, this is your grade, expressed not as a letter but as a number calculated from your credit history and information on your credit report. Basically this score estimates a person's credit risk and provides lenders with a fast, simple way of deciding a person's creditworthiness and making that "lend/don't lend" decision quickly. The credit score is widely used.

What ingredients make up the score?

Five key factors are considered to determine credit scores. The percentages next to each factor below are approximate:

>> **1.** Payment History   35%
>> **2.** Amounts Owed   30%
>> **3.** Length of Credit History   15%
>> **4.** Pattern of Credit Use: 10%
>> **5.** Types of Credit in Use   10%

*Facts from: www.freeecreditreportsearch.com

What's a "good" score?

650 and above: As a rule, a score of 650 or above is very good. A score like this makes it pretty easy for a person to get a credit card or loan and with good terms.

620 to 650: A score between 620 and 650 is respectable, but you may have to provide additional information to your lender or creditor.

Below 620: To lenders, a score below 620 may be considered a "credit risk" (someone who may not be able to repay borrowed money). A low score can complicate the process of getting a credit card or loan, or it might mean very high interest rates.

Your Rating: Depending on who you talk to, your credit rating is just another name for your credit score.

Your History: Yes, everything except your baby pictures. Well, almost ... This is a record of all of your credit information from the day you started using your first credit card or first borrowed money from an institution. Credit reporting agencies (discussed later) collect all relevant information in the form of a "credit report."

Your credit history hangs around for a long time. It is very hard (sometimes nearly impossible) to change. You can't just click your heels together and make your bad credit history vanish, so do all you can keep your credit history clean.

There are only three ways to recover:

>> 1. Change your spending and payment habits.

>> 2. Pay off everything you owe to creditors.

>> 3. Wait, wait, wait. As time passes (lots of time, unfortunately!), your new history will come to the foreground. And don't forget #1!

From a friend, a radio commercial, or a newspaper ad, you'll hear about a company that claims to "erase" or "clean up" bad credit history. Sounds too good to be true! Often these outfits are illegal. They're scams to rip you off and take your money.

"Where Can I Get My Credit Score, Rating, and History?"

Not too long ago. this information was available only to credit agencies and other financial institutions, but recently it became available to the public. You can get your score, rating, and history on the Internet or through your personal credit company. It's a really good idea to check your information every once in a while. After all, it's YOUR history! What does it say about you, and what can you do to possibly improve it?

"Ooops! I see an error . . ."

Take care of it as soon as you can! Write to one of these credit agencies and explain politely your situation, the problem, and your suggested solution.

Equifax Complaint Department
P.O. Box 740241
Atlanta, GA 30374
1800- 685-1111

Esperian Complaint Department
P.O. Box 2002
Allen, TX 75013
888-397-3742

Trans Union Complaint Department
P.O. Box 1000
Chester, PA 19022
800-916-8800

TILL DEBT DO YOU PART

If you're drowning in unpaid bills, there are nonprofit organizations that will give you financial advice and help you improve your credit. Here are a few:

>> Consumer Credit Counseling Service. Call 1-800-388-2227, or visit www.nfcc.org to find the nearest CCCS office.

>> For one-on-one counseling and advice over the phone, call 1-800-680-DEBT, or visit www.myvesta.org.

>> The National Foundation for Consumer Credit has offices in all 50 states. Call 1-800-388-2227 to find the nearest office, or check www.debthelpnow.com.

Caution: Getting one of these companies to negotiate on your behalf may look bad to other companies because it tells them you have credit problems. So, these nonproift organizations can be helpful, but it is possible that using them can also hurt you.

DON'T JUST CUT 'EM UP!

You're spending too much. You found a better card. Whatever the reason, you shouldn't just cut up your old card. Cutting it up is the first step, but not the only step. When you want to get rid of your card for good, you have to cancel it.

Call the number on the back of your card or statement.

(Some companies may require you to write them a letter.) When you call, be ready to provide information that verifies your identify. They might ask you:

>> Your mother's maiden name
>> Your social security number
>> Why you are canceling

TIPS FOR USING CREDIT CARDS

Here are a few tips for using credit cards responsibly:

>> Limit the amount of credit cards you own
(two should be plenty).
>> Get rid of all the cards you don't use. Cut them up, but make sure you cancel them as well.
>> If you move around a lot, try not to change your billing address. Creditors can't stand nomads.
>> Avoid changing jobs frequently. Creditors see this as instability, a liability that can affect your credit.
>> Keep your cards in a safe place.
>> Never lend your card to anyone.
>> Give your credit card information over the phone or Internet ONLY when you're placing an order with a reputable company.
>> Report questionable charges ASAP.
>> Keep all your receipts, and compare them with your monthly statement.
>> Always make payments on time and (when possible) in full. Always exceed the minimum payment!

>> Don't apply for cards you don't need.
>> Get a card with a l-o-n-g grace period.

"Cool" Tip (actually, a Frozen Tip guaranteed to stop impulsive buying): Take your credit cards, put them in a cup of water, and leave them in the freezer. It forces you to wait for the water to thaw out during that next impulsive urge!

THE WRAP

Repeat after me: "Credit cards are my friends."

Hope we haven't made credit cards out to be scary enemies. They're not ... if you have the discipline to use them correctly. It's not the card, it's YOU. Control your spending, make your payments in full and on time, and you will stay out of trouble. Keep in mind this is information we found helpful. It's not everything there is to know about credit cards, and we are not trying to provide any legal advice because we are not lawyers. There's always more to learn. In the words of Spiderman:

WITH GREAT POWER COMES GREAT RESPONSIBILITY.

A credit card holds a lot of power. It can change your life. Are you ready for the responsibility of a credit card? If not, don't get one. It's not worth the risk.

My "To Do" List:

❏ Realize that using a credit card is like taking out a loan.

❏ Think before I swipe. Is it a need, or is it a want?

❏ Look at the terms and conditions carefully.

❏ Consider getting a secured card.

❏ Recognize that reapplying can harm my credit history.

❏ Always check my bill.

❏ Don't pay up-front fees for a credit card.

❏ Know my limit ... and my card's limit.

❏ Maintain a good credit score, rating, and history.

❏ If I no longer want or need my card, cancel it. Don't just cut it up.

❏ Realize that free credit counseling help is available.

❏ Always try to pay in full and on time!

"Cool Stuff" I need to take note of:

_____

_____

_____

_____

_____

_____

_____

_____

_____

Make a Good Impression!

How do you want to be remembered?

FIRST IMPRESSION

1...2...3... BANG

1...2...3... That's how long it takes for someone to get an impression of you. You don't even need to open your mouth ... people are already judging you. Believe it or not, a first impression can last years—sometimes your entire life!

Get the importance of making a good first impression? Even if you screw up a little later on, your good first impression is what's going to be remembered. On the other hand, a bad first impression is a burden you will have to work really hard to change.

Kyle: *Remember that time we hit Mr. Ackland with the ball? Man, did we make an impression on him!*

Kent: *Yeah, the impression of a rugby ball on his face! To make matters worse, we hadn't even been introduced to him yet. Our parents told us to wait patiently at his door; they would be there in a moment, and then all four of us could knock on the door and* *introduce ourselves. Well, while we were waiting, we uh ...*

Kyle: *Well... We were supposed to "wait patiently"—weren't those Dad's exact words? Anyway, while we were waiting, we started kicking the rugby ball around in Mr. Ackland's front yard. One kick was way off and landed right on our neighbor's head as he opened the door! Looking back, I think it would have better if we had broken his window.*

Kent: *Amen! It took nearly a year before he finally realized we weren't as bad as the first impression we'd made! And Kyle, just to clear things up, it was YOUR kick, not mine, that hit Mr. Ackland.*

> ## 2K TIP
>
> **PASS IT ON.** Look for opportunities to help out others. Offer a hand to help a mate with their homework, share chores, wash their car, etc. And don't ask for a favor in return. Instead, ask that they pass it on by doing a good deed for someone else.

So, what are the ingredients to making a good first impression? Read on, and we'll tell you...

CHEESE!

Smile! It's the first thing people like about you! And smiling isn't hard either. In fact, it takes less effort and uses fewer muscles than frowning. How much easier it is to make a good first impression when your facial expressions suggest you're enjoying the moment.

A smile can say a lot about you. It shows other people:

>> **You're a happy person.** Better than a grump! Who doesn't like a happy person? Be happy ... be liked.

>> **You're approachable.** A smile welcomes others. It shows that you won't bite ... that they can talk to you. You'll meet more people if you look approachable and happy.

>> **You're interested.** When you're talking to others, don't you prefer it when they're smiling back at you? It's a good feeling, so why not share it with others? A smile shows you're interested in them and what they have to say. If you make someone else feel good, they're bound to do the same for you.

>> **You're confident.** A smile shows you're comfortable with your surroundings—and with yourself! Think about this: How many people smile when they're nervous?

Kyle: *I remember when we went to Jared's college enrollment day a few years ago. It was his first year there, so he didn't know anyone. As he walked around the campus and the administration room (office), Jared had a grin from ear to ear—not a cheesy one but a genuine smile.*

What amazed me were the people's reactions. In most cases, they responded with a smile and often sparked up a conversation. He began the day not knowing anyone, but in a very short time, he had made a number of new friends. I was also amazed when I saw how the teachers and receptionists seemed to give him more attention and help than the other students. Not only did his smile attract new friends, it got him extra help and made others grin and feel good too!

Do you see how important it is to show your happiness? How could you go wrong? Put a smile on your dial every once in a while ... or as often as possible!

BREAK THE ICE!

Lucky us ... We've been the "new kids" at different schools many, many times. That makes for LOTS of awkward moments around people we didn't know. The sad thing is, there was no real reason for our discomfort. It didn't need to happen.

It seemed every time a teammate would show us around school, he'd stop to say "hi" to someone but would forget to introduce us. There we'd be, standing uncomfortably, shuffling our feet, and clearing our throats. Finally, we'd introduce ourselves. Now, we're not shy. We don't mind

making our own introductions, but it's just not cool when the person you're talking with is someone you don't know and your mate fails to break the ice.

You can bet we learned from "being there" so often. Whenever you're in this situation, think of the other person. Introduce your friend immediately. He or she will definitely have more respect for you.

Tip 1: Sometimes you need to break the ice with your own pick. When you're on your own, or your friend has forgotten about you, it's up to you. Introduce yourself. But don't wait too long! We found the more time that goes by, the more awkward things get. Moral: Don't be shy, and don't wait forever.

Tip 2: When you meet someone for a second time, use your name when you introduce yourself. "Hey, Frank, how are you? It's Kent." Don't put all the pressure on them to remember your name. How many times have you wished people had done this for you? Spare them the embarrassment. Tell them your name ... they'll love you for it.

BE CLOTHES-MINDED

Your smile does a lot of talking for you. So do your clothes. Your clothes say A LOT about who you are and how you're trying to appear. Think about your friends, for example. Doesn't the type of clothes they wear suit their personality? In most cases, it's a pretty clear reflection. Whether you like T-shirts, collared shirts, no shirts, baggy pants, tight pants, no pants—whatever your style, you should consider how other people are going to interpret your image. Yes, it is important to have your own style, to be independent and worry-free, but think before you launch an attack on your wardrobe.

Think, for example, of some of the things you should take into account:

>> **Your audience.** Who are you going to associate with? Parents, teachers, employers, friends, foreigners, ...?

>> **Your purpose.** Are you presenting to your class, going to a party, applying for a job? For an interview, stay away from the casual look and bright colors. If you mean business, you should reflect business in your clothes.

2K TIP

FREE MONEY! Check out and apply for scholarships. There are tons of grants and scholarships available in most school systems. Many go unclaimed. Apply for them. What do you have to lose?

>> **Time of day.** If you hang out at the beach during the day, you should probably get out of your salty, sandy swimsuit before going anywhere! Keep dress code in mind. And note that some facilities change the dress code as the day goes on.

>> **Time of year.** If you like wearing sandals and tank tops in the middle of winter, great. But remember: Even if you're comfortable, others may question your intelligence.

>> **Local culture.** It may not be wise to walk around downtown New York dressed like you're ready to jump on your horse and rope a bull. Where you are makes a massive difference. From our experience, we know how the U.S. varies from state to state and even city to city. Consider your surroundings.

Kyle: *When we were living in New Zealand, it didn't take us long to discover that it was okay to walk everywhere barefoot. It was acceptable downtown, in grocery stores, and even in restaurants. But when we traveled to Australia for vacation, I wasn't allowed to enter* some restaurants because I was wearing flip-flop sandals. (And they were my best ones too!) I learned very quickly that flip-flops were not "shoes" in Australia. Then we came to California; some restaurants post signs saying "Shoes required" or "No shirt, no shoes, no service." The funny thing is, in California, "shoes" CAN be flip-flops. Go figure ... All cultures are different, so be prepared.

BE ON TIME

First impressions are often won or lost in the timing, and if your timing is off, then you're off too. Keeping people waiting is not cool, especially the first time you meet them. So, do your absolute best to arrive on time.

> "Cool Stuff"
>
> IF YOU'RE NOT PUNCTUAL,
> YOU'RE NOT FUNCTIONAL.

Remember: 8a.m. means 8a.m. Not 8:01a.m. or 8:30a.m. and definitely not 10a.m. Do you like to wait around for people who are late and then listen to their excuses? Of course not. So don't put others through it. It doesn't really matter how "legitimate" your excuse is. Allow time for traffic, accidents, or car problems. And if worse comes to worse and you know you're going to be late, even only by a few minutes, call and let them know. It is an easy way to demonstrate you are responsible.

Our coach in New Zealand worked an hour and a half away from where we practiced—and he was never late to training! Sometimes he arrived half an hour early just because he allowed extra time. Naturally, this gave the team no excuse to be late. If he could always be on time with his long commute, we had no reason to be late from only five miles away.

He never accepted any excuses. At the time, it seemed kind of harsh. Looking back, we now realize he was right. If you're organized, being on time shouldn't be a problem. Coaches and employers can read your enthusiasm and dedication through your punctuality.

THE HANDSHAKE

A bad handshake is like grabbing a dead fish and trying to shake life into it. How impressive is that? It's like shaking a cooked noodle. No way!

We've never met a successful person who does not have a (note the key word) *firm* grasp. A handshake plays a huge part in making a good impression because it is one of the first things you do when meeting someone. Like a picture, a handshake is worth a thousand words. A firm one reflects confidence, whereas a dead-fish grip might show that you don't care. It's up to you. How do you want to be remembered?

EYE CONTACT

Having a staring contest with the ground or the nearest wall will NOT impress anyone, and you probably won't win either. It's quite the opposite! Look other people straight in the eye. Show them you are confident with yourself and interested in what they have to say (even if you're not). It also works when you are doing the talking. Looking people in the eye will keep them interested in what you have to say. Isn't it hard to trust what people are saying when they are talking to you while staring off into space?

REMEMBER NAMES

People love the sound of their names! Not many things are more impressive than calling people by name when you greet or leave them. It is way too easy to meet someone, hear them tell you their name, but have it go in one ear and out the other.

Not only is it a plus for the other person, it relieves you of a potentially awkward situation when it comes time to say goodbye or say hello the next time. Make the effort to remember people's names. You'll avoid the awkwardness of ...

"Heyyyyyy . . . uhhhh . . . hi!"

People might think that you don't care enough about them to remember. Think back to times when people couldn't remember your name. How did you feel?

Lots of techniques can help you remember names. Try this: When you hear someone's name, think of something ridiculous that either rhymes with or reminds you of that person. For example, if you meet someone named "Frank," make a mental picture of him dressed up like a "ball-park frank." The more ridiculous it is, the easier it will be to remember. Some people say pictures are the glue of the mind. We agree. It is a lot easier for the human brain to remember comical pictures than words or letters.

An older friend of ours was hired as a bartender for a company's party. Throughout the night, he made an effort to remember details about the guests, including their names, of course. As the party went on, not only was he able to call each guest by first name, but he remembered each person's favorite drink so he could have a fresh one ready when they finished the last one. By the end of the party, he made several hundred dollars in tips—clearly because of the attention he gave the guests. As everyone began to leave, he said good-bye to each guest using her or his name. Everyone was extremely impressed. And it didn't end there: He received so many referrals that he was booked solid for the next few months.

The bottom line: People love it when you can call them by their names because it shows interest and effort. They feel special. As a result, they'll treat you with more respect too.

HYGIENE?

Yes, hygiene! This is one thing you just can't afford to overlook. You may have the trendiest clothes, the best posture, and natural conversation skills, but if your clothes are dirty, your breath stinks, or you reek of body odor (sorry—we just had to be honest), your positive attributes will be quickly forgotten.

Odor can make you blind. Let us explain. It's hard to see what a person is doing well or concentrate on what they are saying when you are holding your breath because of the odor! Lack of oxygen to the brain does not improve awareness.

Okay, let's get serious. Even your friends may not tell you if you have a hygiene problem. In most cases, people don't want to take the risk of offending someone. What does this mean? It's all you baby! In most cases, you'll be the only one to look after yourself.

Your personal hygiene is key to making a good impression. If others are not enjoying your presence, chances are you are not going to leave a good impression. Just because you may be immune to your own "brand" doesn't mean everyone else is too. Below is a list of tips you can use to stay on top of your game:

>> Brush your teeth daily.
>> Carry breath mints, spray, or drops.
>> Take showers regularly!
>> Use deodorant. It's a need, not a want!
>> Wear clean clothes. Wash your clothes after you wear them. Recycling is cool, but in this case, how about using the spin cycle ... if you know what we mean.

MEET THE PARENTS

Parents are curious people. They like to know who their kids hang out with. When it comes time to meet them, don't be shy. Be yourself. Carry on a conversation; they won't hurt you (most of the time). Parents love to be acknowledged and spoken to, because most teens don't make the effort to chat. When you do, you'll stand out and be remembered.

When you meet them for the first time, chances are you'll be at their house. But that doesn't mean you need to wait for them to come to you. You can be the first to introduce yourself. Be the guest with the best, and use your manners. Make the effort to smile so you come across like you're enjoying yourself—even if all you can think about is saying "Good-bye. It was nice talking to you."

This is especially true when you meet your girlfriend's (or your boyfriend's) parents. Here, a relationship IS important. Take the time to acknowledge his or her parents, and apply what you're going to learn in People Skills, the next chapter.

PROFESSOR WHO?

No, you do NOT want to have a bad relationship with teachers. It only makes your life harder. We know you've seen students struggle through school because they had poor relationships with their teachers.

Now we know you don't want to be the teacher's pet. (Neither do we.) But we can still learn something from them. You see, teachers' pets have figured out the importance of making a good impression—and they're benefiting from it. You have to admit, the kids who befriend their teachers have an advantage over everyone else. Wouldn't you agree?

Those of you who have really good relationships with your teachers know what we're talking about. It's nice, isn't it? And it's not hard to do. I mean, let's face it, teachers don't go the extra mile for flakes, and the flakes don't go the extra mile for teachers. In any case, we all need to remember that teachers are in a position to have a HUGE impact on our lives.

It's easy to rag on teachers, but let's admit it: They really do have a bigger effect on us than most of us realize. They have provided us with all sorts of important skills we use everyday, such as writing, speaking, math, and endless general knowledge. Collectively, they are our coaches in the game of life. Think of all the little things they do to shape us into the people we are and the people we will ultimately become.

They have played a huge role in shaping your attitude, opinions, and the way you handle situations in your life. Our teachers greatly affect our potential, and if this is the case, don't you want them to influence you for the better and extend your potential? You may not always be able to control this, but you can definitely encourage it. How? By making sure your teachers are impressed with you and therefore want to help you. These days, you sure can't live without them—so you might as well make your life easier by befriending them.

Miss B: *As a teacher, I know how important it is for students to create a good relationship with their instructors. From the first day in my class, Kent and Kyle made an effort to make (and keep) a good impression, create conversation with me, get their work in on time, and try hard to earn the best grade possible—and I noticed it. Often,* *they were traveling or at sports events. Because I respected them so much, when they asked for an extension or had to turn in late assignments, it was the fact that I knew they had integrity that made me want to extend the exception to them.*

Kent and Kyle: *Thank you, Miss B.*

Back in the day, students would bring apples for their teachers. Today, it's a dead tradition. So develop your own new ones. Remember the old saying, "An apple a day keeps the doctor away"? Well, in this case, it goes something like this, "An apple a day keeps an 'F' away." Do the little things that keep your teachers happy with you, and your school life will be a lot more enjoyable.

We asked a number of teachers what they liked to see from students. The list below is *theirs!*

CHOOSE YOUR BATTLES. Certain arguments are not worth fighting. Before you start choking the other person, ask yourself, "How important is this to me?" Even if you "win," what will you really accomplish? Learn to let the smaller battles slide by. Keep your cool.

>> Be punctual. Lateness is a form of communicating without words. It shows lack of interest—and that REALLY annoys teachers! This also goes for assignments. Get them in on time!

>> Use the name they prefer. Is it "Doctor Weston"? "Miss Weston"? "Ms."? "Mrs."? Or does she prefer "Betty"? The choice, of course, belongs to the teachers. If you don't know, then ask.

>> Show the right attitude. Teachers notice this quickly. School is an opportunity. Just ask kids from other countries who must work whether they consider school an opportunity. Be genuine, and be thankful for your opportunity here.

>> Don't be a number in the class. Be who you are. Participate! Be the student who is remembered, not the one who is happily forgotten.

>> Don't be a grade grubber. If you feel a grade is unfair or you don't understand how a grade was determined, ask. But don't nag to get a higher grade or nitpick about a few points here and there!

>> Use positive body language. Show that you are alive, alert, participating. Your posture and facial expressions often speak "louder than words." Besides, don't do this just for the teacher—do it for you! You'll need this skill in your career.

>> Offer positive feedback. Let teachers know when they are doing well. When you benefit from a lecture, learn something worthwhile from the discussion, or improve a skill because of an assignment, let the teacher know—but not just to score points. It helps teachers evaluate their instruction.

Are you doing everything you can to make a good impression?

THE WRAP

Little things go a long way. People do notice and will remember them. If you make an effort to leave a good impression, people will return the favor and treat you well too. You'll stick out from the crowd and be extraordinary, because most people don't do little things that make a huge difference. "Go the extra mile" and make these qualities habits, because the difference between "ordinary" and "extraordinary" is just a little bit extra.

My "To Do" List:

☐ Smile.

☐ Break the ice. Introduce my friends and, in some cases, myself.

☐ Pay attention to my body language. Do I like what it says about me?

☐ Be clothes-minded.

☐ Be on time.

☐ Give a firm handshake.

☐ Make eye contact.

☐ Remember names.

☐ Maintain healthy hygiene.

☐ Talk to parents (mine and my friends).

☐ Make the effort to create a good relationship with my teachers.

"Cool Stuff" I need to take note of:

_____

_____

_____

_____

_____

_____

_____

_____

_____

People Skills

12

Make your positive impression last.

PEOPLE SKILLS

We devoted an entire chapter to making a good impression. It's that important! But it's even more important to keep the reputation you earned.

Think of someone who makes you feel special and appreciated. What does she do that makes you feel that way? Now think about someone who everyone likes. Why does he consistently get that response?

We wondered too! So we did the research, and we have found that ...

IT'S ALL ABOUT OTHERS

This is possibly the most valuable skill of all. Unless you want to be a hermit and live in the woods entirely by yourself, you'll have to make an effort to treat others how you want to be treated:

> THE WAY TO MAKE A GOOD FIRST IMPRESSION IS TO SHOW OTHER PEOPLE THAT YOU ARE IMPRESSED WITH THEM!
>
> —J.R. Parrish

Bull's-eye! When you focus your positive energy towards others (rather than on *you, you, you*), you'll find things start going your way. If you are meeting someone for the first time, wouldn't you get a good impression of them if they gave you the best seat, asked for your opinion, or complimented you? Of course you would. Focus on others. Let them go first, shine the spotlight on them, and let them know they are important to you. Remember, little gestures leave lasting positive impressions.

LIVE UP TO YOUR WORD

One way to keep that positive first impressions is to live up to your word. What an excellent way to highlight your first impression! It's real simple. If you said you're going to do something ... do it! Do it well ... and on time! If it's a simple task, just get it done. If it requires you to go the extra mile, then put in that extra effort.

How many times have you said you'd call someone ... and didn't? Yes, this simple task is an example of living up to your word. Make the call!

You told a friend you'd call by 8p.m. with some information — it doesn't matter what!. If you don't have the info by 8p.m., call anyway! "Hey, I don't have that number, address, or (*fill in the blank*) yet, but I'm still working on it. I'll call you as soon as I get it."

Don't you get frustrated when people don't do what they say they're going to do? It sure annoys us! Your word should mean a lot not only to you but to others too.

"I FORGOT!" "I FORGOT!"

Great excuse. (Hardly original.) Did you really think it got you off the hook? No, it does not matter how good you think your excuse may be.

> *"Cool Stuff"*
>
> PEOPLE DON'T WANT TO HEAR EXCUSES; THEY WANT RESULTS!

In the real world, you need to remember things. Write a note to yourself on your day planner or your calendar. Tying a string around your finger? Do whatever works for you ... just don't make excuses.

Danielle: *I used to have a big problem remembering things. It got to the point that no one could rely on me to get things done. Not only did I feel bad, I was embarrassed. I would often forget to call someone, send an e-mail, or get a task done that I said I would. I originally thought that it wasn't my fault because my life was so hectic. I always had way too much going on, and it was extremely difficult to manage it all. But I soon realized most people don't care how busy you are or how little time you have—even if the reasons are legitimate in your mind. Like Kent and Kyle say, people want results. They want to see an outcome, not hear reasons why something wasn't done.*

I couldn't afford to forget anymore, so I started to do everything I could to remind myself of the things I used to overlook. I now carry a little notepad and pen with me all the time. I have a dry-erase board set up on the wall in my room. I constantly set the alarm on my cell phone. And I stick Post-it Notes in places I always look. Now, I seldom forget anything. Not only have I regained people's trust, I have also made my life MUCH easier and a lot less stressful.

"LIAR LIAR!"

No one wants the reputation of being a liar—terrible to live with and nearly impossible to get rid of. Make a conscious effort never to lie or stretch the truth. It may make your story a little more interesting, it may make you look cool at the moment, it may get you a laugh, but lying will come back and bite you — hard! And most of the time your lying bites you without you knowing it. When people find out you lied, they generally won't confront you. They won't call you a liar. Instead, they just won't believe anything you say from then on, and they may tell others about your lying!

Do you know pathological liars? We do. They're so used to "extending the truth" that they don't even realize they do it anymore.

They are nice people and they have good intentions, but whenever they tell a story or say they're going to do something, we find it hard to believe them. They have developed a habit of lying (yes, it is a habit). Their "word" is meaningless; after all, we can never be sure it is the truth. Make sure your life doesn't follow the example of the boy who cried "wolf."

LISTEN UP!

LISTEN UP!

It's easy to talk too much (another habit). Most people who do, forget to listen. What impresses you more: A motor mouth or an intensive listener? Clue: The answer is NOT "motor mouth."

When you listen, people notice. They notice because most of us don't listen well. So when you pay attention, you'll immediately stand out and be noticed. Not only does it show self-control, it shows the speaker that you care. Then work at trying to remember what you hear. When you can recall what someone said, you prove that you listened and—yes!—you will make a good impression.

Kent: *Before I left for New Zealand, I was talking to a friend who was excited about getting a car. I wasn't able to talk to him for a few months, but when we finally did talk, the first thing I asked him about was his car. He was thrilled I made the effort to remember and really appreciated it. Remembering important things about other people's lives always makes them feel good. And when you can make other people feel good... you'll feel good too!*

SHOW INTEREST ...
ASK QUESTIONS

We're not talking about those filler questions like "So ... how 'bout them Lakers, huh?" We mean asking genuine questions relevant to what the speaker is talking about. Have you ever carried on a conversation with someone who just says, "Yep... uh huh... right... mmmm..."? How does it make you feel? Most people think the "listener" just doesn't care about what they're saying. Is that "leaving a good impression"? Hardly.

When someone is talking to you, use body language that shows you're paying attention. Look and act interested. Isn't that what you want when you're talking to others? Remember that the key to making a good impression is to show other people that you are interested in them. One of the best ways to do this is by asking questions—about them and their message. When you ask questions, you're showing you care.

> "Cool Stuff"
>
> WHEN YOU MAKE OTHERS FEEL APPRECIATED, THEY WILL APPRECIATE YOU.

DON'T LOOK FOR FRIENDS ...
BE A FRIEND

> "Cool Stuff"
>
> IN ORDER TO FIND A FRIEND, YOU MUST FIRST BE A FRIEND.

Tessa: *Like Kent and Kyle, I attended many different high schools. I had the opportunity of finding what works and what doesn't when it comes to making new friends. Sometimes I really screwed up, and sometimes I found ways that really worked well. And now, I can basically narrow it down to one thing.*

*When I changed schools this one particular time, I made the mistake of **looking for friends**. From day one, I was searching for people I thought I could be friends with. But to my disappointment, I didn't find any. I couldn't figure out why. By the end of the week, nothing had changed, so I decided that I better try something else.*

*This time I set out to **be a friend**, meaning I went out of my way to be nice to everyone. I made an effort to listen to them, ask them questions, and just be considerate. Almost instantly, I noticed a huge difference. I found that people want to be around others who want to be a friend, not those who are only looking for friends. When I realized this, I discovered that there were friends around me the entire time.*

What's the moral of the story? You can't simply get friends. **You make them by giving of yourself, not by looking for them.** *You have to be a friend in order to find friends.*

TAME YOUR
EGO

Kyle: *The Gudauskas brothers, three of my good friends, are world-class surfers. As a result of their accomplishments, they are greatly respected. They'd be respected for their accomplishments even if they were cocky or arrogant. But because they're really down to earth and genuine, they've gained a level of respect even beyond their "accomplishments."*

> DON'T LET YOUR EGO GET IN THE WAY
> OF YOUR SUCCESS.
>
> —Pete Cutino

When things are going really well, our reality can get clouded and our ego takes over. Ever notice that in other people? Ever notice that in yourself?

Sometimes, we (as humans) suspect that acting arrogantly makes other people believe we're even better than our accomplishments. This is a great example of irony, because the natural reaction of those around us is quite the opposite. People get sick of inflated egos, and eventually even the respect for accomplishments will fade away.

Bet on this: When you act modestly, you'll get more admiration and praise. Strange, but downplaying yourself and your achievements gets you much further than boasting and bragging. Keep it all on the down low.

When people discover your accomplishments on their own, without you telling them, it gives your achievement much more significance. It's okay to feel proud of yourself; just don't broadcast or announce your successes. No one wants to hear or see how good you think you are! Allow them find out for themselves.

LET YOUR ACTIONS SPEAK FOR YOU.
YOU'LL FIND THEY SPEAK MUCH LOUDER
THAN YOU EVER COULD.

MANNERS?
MANNERS!

DON'T RESERVE YOUR BEST BEHAVIOR FOR
SPECIAL OCCASIONS. YOU CAN'T HAVE
TWO SETS OF MANNERS, TWO SOCIAL CODES
— ONE FOR THOSE YOU ADMIRE AND
WANT TO IMPRESS, ANOTHER FOR THOSE
WHOM YOU CONSIDER UNIMPORTANT.
YOU MUST BE THE SAME TO ALL PEOPLE.

—*Lillian Eichler Watson*

Don't cringe—and don't you DARE close the book! Yes, we're gonna talk about manners. Good manners might get you more than you think. Practicing correct etiquette might benefit you in several ways:

>> More friends
>> Better relationships
>> Higher self-esteem
>> Favors
>> More respect from others

Good manners means more than not wiping your mouth with your sleeve at a fine restaurant or drinking from the dog's bowl when no one is looking. But if that's been your style, don't worry! Practicing correct etiquette ain't hard ... if you're aware of your actions and willing to change. Once you make new habits, you're set for life.

GOOD MANNERS WILL OPEN DOORS THAT THE BEST EDUCATION CANNOT.

—Justice Clarence Thomas, U.S. Supreme Court

Still struggling with this issue? Look at it this way: Good manners are like a beautiful beach where everyone wants to be. Bad ones are like a dump no one wants to go near. Make a decision NOW to use the manners you have and seek to learn more.

"Cool Stuff"

THE BEHAVIOR YOU DECIDE TO USE THROUGHOUT LIFE WILL DETERMINE HOW OTHER PEOPLE TREAT YOU.

It's very important to create good manners, because bad ones can cost you a lot!

>> Talking with your mouth full and dropping food on your lap . . .
Cost: $40 for those nice pants you just ruined

>> Picking your nose at a business meeting and getting fired . . .
Cost: Your $50,000-a-year salary (Ouch!)

>> Pretending the potato on your fork is an airplane (sound effects included) on your first date. **Cost:** $60 for dinner ... and now dateless

>> Investing your time into learning good manners ... **Priceless!**

DO ~~THEY~~
LIKE IT?

One of the best ways to leave a good impression is to find what people like and then do it. This may sound "schmoozy" but it's really not. You probably already do some of this without realizing it.

How do you find out what other people like? Try these:

>> **1. Listen**. Look for hints and clues in what people say. Look for key words like "I love it when people..." Now all you have to do is remember what they say and apply it. This is like gift shopping. You don't know what to buy your sister for her birthday, so you pay attention to what she says, what she likes, and what she comments about. Then buying her a gift is easy! It's the same here. Listen ... then you'll know what people like. You can't go wrong.

>> **2. Observe.** How do people handle situations with other people? Their actions and expressions can speak volumes. By observing carefully, you can avoid the embarrassment, hassle, or frustration of doing

something that irritates other people. Watch how those around you react to others. Look at their body language; observe the frowns, smiles, eye-rolling, or tense body language.

FACE TO FACE. When all your friends are sitting around and they start to talk about someone else—regardless if you agree or not—suggest that they bring up the issue with that person. Talking behind people's backs is low. Keep in mind: Those who gossip to you, will gossip about you.

>> 3. Ask yourself, "What annoys ME?" Chances are, things that annoy you will annoy other people too. Avoid frustrating other people by using the trial-and-error process. Identify pet peeves. It's important to find what people don't like and avoid doing it. Almost everybody has a few pet peeves that just really aggravate them. Look for comments like, "I hate it when people do that" or "Man, that annoys me!" It's valuable information. Whenever you can steer clear of these pet peeves, you'll have a better chance of leaving a good impression.

It also works in reverse. Chances are, things that you like, others will also like. Ask yourself, "What do I like that people do?" Then share those things with others.

The trick to doing these three things successfully is simple: Be aware of how others feel, and remember what you discover.

WRAP

By applying these concepts to your life you'll keep the good impression you made. Remember, these are all fundamentals. You can't win a game without them—especially the game of life. If you remember nothing else from this chapter, remember this: Work at making others feel important. Put them in the spotlight. Make them feel appreciated.

My "To Do" List:

❏ Make others feel special.

❏ Live up to my word.

❏ Ditch the "I forgot" excuse. Remember ... and do it!

❏ Tell the truth ... always.

❏ Listen ... and remember what you've heard.

❏ Show interest in others by asking them questions.

❏ Don't look for friends; be the friend.

❏ Tame your ego.

❏ Use good manners.

❏ Find out what other people like and apply it.

❏ Find out what other people don't like and avoid doing it.

"*Cool Stuff*" I need to take note of:

_____

_____

_____

_____

_____

_____

_____

_____

_____

_____

_____

Communicate Great! 13

Blah blah
blah.

COMMUNICATE
GREAT

In ancient times, cavepeople (how's that for being politically correct?) had no spoken or written language. They communicated through a wide variety of odd signals, gestures, dances, grunts, and groans. The funny thing is, some people today have yet to figure out that mankind has progressed beyond that stage!

You know the type of person we are talking about here. It's not pretty. The thing is, we no longer need to mimic monkeys by jumping up and down and beating our chests to communicate with others—no matter how much you may want to. In fact, it's a good idea not to. How you communicate leaves a lasting impression on everyone you meet, and it can make or break your job, schooling, relationships, blah, blah, blah.

MORE THAN WORDS

Break time: Congratulations!!! We just want to give you a pat on the back for reading this far—good for you! But don't stop now ... some of the most important *"Cool Stuff"* follows.

The words you use, the order you put them in, and the energy you project them with make a huge impression on the people you talk to. In only a short period of time, anyone can learn a lot about a person by the way he or she communicates. Sure, the car you drive or clothes you wear do say something, but they are not nearly as important as your vocabulary, your tone, your body language, and your ability to group your thoughts logically.

Think back to some of the best leaders who ever lived. None of them slouched, slurred their speech, or spoke timidly. Could you imagine if Martin Luther King Jr. stood up in front of millions of people with his head down, shoulders rolled forward, and shyly said, "Ummmm, hey guys ... Like, I have a dream. Cool, huh? Follow me if you want, and everything will be good." Do you think his message would have been very powerful? Definitely not!

If you want people to listen to what you have to say and act upon it, you need to practice. Communication is a combination of art and skill. It takes perseverance to build an impressive vocabulary and develop the ability to get your point across.

How well do you communicate? Most of us underestimate the importance of this critical skill. People will make judgments about your intelligence, employability, honesty, and maturity based on your ability to communicate. So, yes ... it's very important! Let's go through some of the steps that will help you improve your communication skill.

First, we need to know what makes a great communicator great! (Make sense? Good.) Question: If asked to name a "famous great speaker," who is the first person you think of?

"Cool Stuff" COMMUNICATE concept

Step 1: Select five people who you think are great speakers or communicators. They can be famous or maybe just your neighbors. (There is no wrong or right answer!)

Step 2: Next to each name, list (briefly) the reasons why you think he or she communicates well. What are the attributes that make each person great?

Person 1: _____

Reason: _____

_____

_____

Person 2: _____

Reason: _____

_____

_____

Person 3: _____

Reason: _____

_____

_____

Person 4: _____

Reason: _____

_____

_____

Person 5: _____

Reason: _____

_____

_____

Step 3: Look over your list, and circle any recurring words. The qualities you circle are things you should focus on when you communicate.

A BACKGROUND CHECK ...

Basically, the word *communicate* means "to share something with another person." Let's break it down:

>> **com-** (like *co-*, *con-*, and *cor-*) means "with." (Just think of chili CON carne, "chili WITH meat.")

>> And **-muni-** comes from *munus*, "a gift" or something you share. (Look up the words *munificent* and *community*, for example.)

In other words, when you communicate, you share something with someone else!

Remember when your teachers talked about "language arts"? Well, they were referring to speaking, reading, writing, and listening. But speaking, reading, writing, and listening aren't the ONLY ways we communicate.

You know that look your mom or dad gives you whenever

you're really late, or when you forgot to do something? (Don't you hate when that happens?) They don't need any words to communicate their feelings. We all know exactly what those faces mean, don't we? Those expressions say absolutely everything we need to know.

THE SILENT LANGUAGE

Body language speaks volumes! It actually speaks to your listener before you get a chance to open your mouth. Therefore, the way you carry yourself does the initial talking. Do you like what your body language is saying about you?

Here is one concept we must understand:

> "Cool Stuff"
>
> OUR COMMUNICATION SKILLS AND THE WAY WE PRESENT OURSELVES WILL DETERMINE HOW OTHERS TREAT US.

Most of what others see depends on the way we carry ourselves. If you stand like you're lacking confidence or certainty, you are sending that message loud and clear to everyone who looks at you. As a result, they'll treat you accordingly.

You may not even get the chance to know a person because

he or she has already branded you as insecure, anxious, or nervous. But don't worry. Once you habitually use positive body language, you create the opportunity to impress others even before you meet them. How cool is that?

Here are some tips to getting off to the right start:

>> Put your shoulders back.
>> Open up your stance (but not too much). This will show that you are approachable and have nothing to hide.
>> Stand tall.
>> Keep your head up and your ears over your shoulders.
>> Look people directly in the eye (wandering eyes can make you look insecure).
>> Smile. (Yes, it's part of good body language.)

2K TIP

LEAVE 'EM SOME. What do you think you're worth? When it comes time to leave a tip, ask yourself, "How much would I give myself for a similar effort?" Don't be stingy. If the waiter or waitress did a good job ... give a little extra. Put yourself in their shoes.

Here's what you need to stay away from (unless you are trying to give the wrong impression):

>> Crossing your arms
>> Looking at the floor and keeping your head down
>> Keeping your hands in your pockets
>> Frowning. (Are you looking for sympathy?)
>> Slouching and rolling your shoulders forward
>> Popping your knuckles. To a lot of people this is very irritating.
>> Constantly jiggling your keys or spare change, constantly tapping a pen, constantly fondling your cell phone—or, for that matter, any other equally annoying distraction!
>> Dragging your feet

SPEAKING: WHAT, WHEN, WHO, AND HOW

What you say, when you say it, whom you say it to, and how you deliver it will make a difference in the way other people respond to you.

What: What you say is extremely important. We've been learning this all of our lives. Ever since we could understand English, we were told what was appropriate and what was unacceptable to say. Whether we found this out from a spanking with the big wooden spoon or soap in our mouths, we now have a fair idea of what's right and wrong.

We know, for instance, that it's not appropriate to walk up to an overweight person and ask, "When is the baby due?" or ask someone, "Do you not like wearing deodorant?"

Before you talk, ask yourself these questions:

>> How can I be more concise and still get my message across clearly?

>> What exactly do I want this person to know?

When: It's all about timing. Telling your dad about your bad grades may be not such a good idea right when he gets home from a long day at work or right after he accidentally backed over the cat. Think about the timing before you open your mouth.

Before you talk, ask yourself these questions:

>> Is this the right time to have a discussion with this person?

>> Does this person have time to talk to me right now?

Who: When a policeman pulls you over, it wouldn't be wise to ask for a donut. Tell your teacher how much you dislike her class? I don't think so! Certain words, thoughts, or phrases are not appropriate for everyone. Consider whom you're speaking with prior to blurting out the first thing that comes into your head.

Before you talk, ask yourself these questions:

>> What would be the most diplomatic way to express my thoughts and not offend this person?

>> What phrasing would be most appropriate for the person I'm speaking to?

DJ YOU. We all have songs that make us feel good. Use your favorite tunes to pump yourself up when you feel down. There's just not enough time in life to mope around. Get pumped!

How: A girl you know puts on a bit too much makeup. Which of the following comments do you think will work better?

>> "You look much prettier with less makeup."

>> "Gee, look who fell in the makeup pot."

There are many ways to say the same thing. In the end, it's up to you. But in most cases, putting your ideas in a positive light will get you further.

Before you talk, ask yourself these questions:

>> How do I want this person to react to what I am about to say?

>> How should I respond to topics that might be brought up?

If you master What/When/Who/How, others will want to talk to you and will be interested in what you have to say. A good communicator is able to keep anyone's interest, no matter what the topic.

THE SPACE BETWEEN
YOUR THOUGHTS

Some people think the faster they talk, the better. Not true. Get your thoughts together before you speak. This seems obvious, but from time to time, all of us have blurted something out that makes no sense at all or can't be understood, and then people look at us like we're from a different planet!

In the previous section, "Speaking: What, When, Who, and How," we mentioned the importance of asking yourself a few questions before you put your lips into gear. At first this may seem a little weird, almost like you're stalling, but in reality, if done properly, your message will be clearer, more concise, and more compelling.

Take that split second between your thoughts to organize your ideas. There's no rush! Think! Pause before you speak! Of course, don't give the listener enough time to set up camp and fall asleep.

Tip 1: Use the space between your thoughts and ideas, NOT between each word. Basically ... what ... I'm ... trying ... to ... say ... is ... DON'T DO THIS!

Tip 2: If you really don't have something worthwhile to say, don't overthink, ponder some more, and then bust out a string of 100 sentences about something no one wants to hear anyway. As our uncle always told us, "Never miss an opportunity to be quiet and just listen."

> **"Cool Stuff"**
>
> SOMETIMES YOU'RE BETTER OFF KEEPING YOUR MOUTH SHUT AND LETTING OTHER PEOPLE THINK YOU'RE A FOOL, THAN OPENING YOUR MOUTH AND CONFIRMING IT.

THE "OTHER" PART

When most people think of communication, they think of talking, but there is a much more important part: listening. Most of us don't like to listen. Of course, it is impossible to communicate if no one pays attention. Remember our earlier definition: *Communicate* means "to share something with another person."

Here's something to keep in mind:

> **"Cool Stuff"**
>
> YOU HAVE ONE MOUTH BUT TWO EARS, SO IT'S A GOOD RULE OF THUMB TO LISTEN TWICE AS MUCH AS YOU SPEAK.

A lot of people "hear" but do not "listen." There is a difference. Hearing someone is to know someone is talking, whereas listening is trying to understand and concentrate on what someone is saying. When you're a good listener, you not only hear the message, you also discover what the person's motives are, why they are telling you this in the first place, and what they expect you to do as a result.

In conversations, observe others carefully as you listen. You can pick up on when to say things or when not to, different techniques to explain or describe something, and at the same time, acquire new vocabulary. Be sure to listen and not just hear what is being said. Good listening skills fuel good conversation and communication, which everyone benefits from in the end. If you listen, you'll never say something like this:

> "SHE DUMPED ME. SHE SAID SOMETHING
> ABOUT ME NOT LISTENING
> ... OR SOMETHING.
> I WASN'T REALLY PAYING ATTENTION."

Obviously, listening is not only important for guys. Almost everyone could become a better listener.

Listening tips:

>> Focus on the message, not the messenger.

>> Keep eye contact to avoid getting distracted.

>> Have a pen and paper handy to jot down key points (this helps you remember what is being said AND helps you to focus too).

>> Repeat the speaker's main ideas to yourself (in your head, not aloud).

>> Withhold any negative feelings or emotions.

>> Listen to understand, not to respond.

>> Remain open-minded to new ideas; don't automatically shut down when the topic is uncomfortable.

HOT TOPICS

Be aware of what you talk about. Is it worthwhile? Do other people want to hear about the topics you bring up? One of our friends always talked about himself, his problems, and his successes. That's OK, but it gets old ... fast. The truth is, people get sick of hearing about you, you, you or the same topics over and over. Don't be the person who says, "That's enough from me. Now what do YOU think about ME?" Be versatile. Be open-minded. What you talk about tells others what kind of person you are.

> **"Cool Stuff"**
>
> PEOPLE WITH SMALL MINDS TALK ABOUT OTHERS;
> PEOPLE WITH AVERAGE MINDS TALK ABOUT
> THINGS; AND PEOPLE WITH EXCELLENT MINDS
> TALK ABOUT IDEAS.

SLOW DOWN!

A lot of people live by this phrase: "So much to say ... so little time." When you have a lot to talk about, it's easy to cram as many words as possible into as few seconds as possible. Instead, step back, take control of your mouth, and push the slo-mo button. By doing this, you'll avoid one of the worst conversation killers ... mumbling.

Do you get annoyed when someone talks and talks but you can't understand what he's saying? Don't be afraid to open your mouth and move those lips! Overexaggerate your enunciation if you have to. You won't look as weird as you will feel. Of course, you can also still mumble when you speak slowly, so be careful. The more clearly you speak, the easier it will be for your listener.

Many people have the impression that speaking slower makes you seem uneducated and dim-witted. However, it's quite the opposite. When you speak slowly, you give your listeners a chance to understand what you just said. Downshift your speech to a lower gear, pause after your main points, and remain confident. People will listen to you—and will *want* to listen to you!

PEOPLE RATE SPEAKERS WHO SPEAK MORE SLOWLY AS BEING 38 PERCENT MORE KNOWLEDGEABLE THAN SPEAKERS WHO SPEAK MORE QUICKLY.

—*Peterson, Cannito, and Brown (1995)*

Quoted in David Niven, *The 100 Simple Secrets of Successful People: What Scientists Have Learned and How You Can Use It*. New York: HarperCollins Publishers, 2002, p. 37.

SLANG VS. VOCAB

A lot of what we say and how we say it should depend on whom you're speaking to: your audience. Your parents may tell you to use an extensive vocabulary whenever you speak and "Don't use slang!" The truth is, there is a time and a place for everything. You wouldn't want to talk like  a Shakespearean poet when you're hangin' out casually with your mates. At the same time, it wouldn't be wise to use all the lingo you know around your parents and their friends. There is a balance you have to find.

People will get turned off if you start talkin' all mumbo jumbo, ya know wat I mean? I pity the foo dat don't.

> "Cool Stuff"
>
> KNOW YOUR AUDIENCE AND SPEAK ACCORDINGLY.

Would you dress the same way for a job interview as you would for a day at the beach? We hope not. You already know how important it is to dress appropriately for each occasion, right? Well, just as you dress appropriately, you should also speak appropriately, according to the occasion.

To some degree, you probably already do this. If someone hands you a phone and says, "It's for you." What's the first thought that comes to mind? You'll most likely say, "Who is it?"

Why? Because you first need to know who you'll be talking to—in other words, who is your audience? Before you open your mouth and say, "What's up, dude?" or "Howzit, girlfriend?" you'll want to make sure it's not your principal or a teacher, right?

THE WRAP

Practice communicating by listening intently and describing your ideas in a way that is interesting, clear, and understandable. Remember: Communication involves almost everything you do. It is impossible to live without it. From sports to relationships, the better you are at communicating, the smoother and more enjoyable your life will become.

Some *Cool Stuff* to keep yourself on top of your game:

>> Concentrate on varying your tone; this always makes your message more interesting to your listener.

>> Overexaggerate your lip and jaw movement to make your diction clearer.

>> Subscribe to an online vocabulary-improvement service such as Word of the Day, a superb free service available at www.merriamwebster.com

>> Pay close attention when you see yourself on film. How do you sound? How do you carry yourself? What does your body language say to others? Take advantage of the opportunity to see yourself as others see you.

>> Ask others what you do well and what you could do to improve.

TRY IT. We've been to countries where it's considered rude not to try the local dish, so in those cases, we didn't have much of a choice. We must admit, some of the food looked a little sketchy, but tasted GREAT! It's easy to make an assumption and judge food by its cover. Try it before you say you hate it.

>> Recite tongue twisters. Visit www.geocities.com/Athens/8136/tonguetwisters.html

>> Pay close attention to teachers' comments, and make an effort to apply what they recommend.

My "To Do" List:

❏ Don't communicate like a caveman.
❏ Always maintain positive body language.
❏ Master the What/When/Who/How way of speaking.
❏ Remember that listening is more important than talking.
❏ I must not only hear, but listen too.
❏ Adjust how I speak according to my listener/s.
❏ Slow down! Take my time to gather my thoughts before I open my mouth.
❏ Be aware of what I talk about.
❏ Communicate great!

Back to Your Future

14

The future belongs to
those who prepare
for it today.

—Malcolm X

YOUR FUTURE

The future is closer than we think. It seems far away—so far, we don't need to worry about it. In reality, it is only right around the corner.

In spite of what you may think ...

> *"Cool Stuff"*
>
> YOU ARE NEVER TOO YOUNG TO START DESIGNING YOUR FUTURE.

Planning doesn't start when you decide to buy a house or start a family. In fact, it's the opposite! You can design your future simply by finding what you want from life and learning to make the right decisions, create the right goals, and develop the right habits to get those goals. Planning doesn't have to be a major operation ... *if you start **now!***

FORKS IN THE ROAD

Every decision you make is a fork in the road. Every decision will affect your future and where and how you will end up. Remember, it's impossible to go back in time to change a bad decision, so let's get into the habit of making right decisions now.

PLANNING FOR THE FUTURE IS DOING ANYTHING YOU CAN THAT YOU WILL BENEFIT FROM ONE SECOND FROM NOW, TOMORROW, AND THE REST OF YOUR LIFE.

Life is just one decision after the next. Get out of bed grumpy, or smiling? A decision. Study for a test, or watch TV? A decision. You wouldn't be *where* or *who* you are today if you made different choices yesterday. Sure, every decision has a consequence, but if you choose to avoid them or procrastinate, you'll never be in control of your future. Your decisions will either hold you back or help lead you toward a brighter future. Look at your life realistically, and take charge of the decisions you make.

Our friend Ben didn't like making decisions. He had a happy-go-lucky attitude and figured everything would work out fine in the end. For a long time, it did, but he didn't recognize the overall direction his actions were taking him until he found himself caught up in a big mess.

Ben: *I never took life too seriously, but I should have realized there are certain times when you should. In school, I never worried much about anything. I easily drifted through each grade all the way up to my junior year in high school. My routines soon became habits. I didn't pay much attention to deadlines, report cards, or tips from my friends and family, because I always thought that everything would be all right in the end.*

I was offered opportunities to do extra credit, get additional tutoring, and join study groups in the library but never took advantage of any offer. In the past, whenever I had problems, I would talk to my teachers at the last minute and try to work things out. However, by my junior year, my own foot was kicking me in the butt. I failed a couple of important tests and just kept my fingers crossed, hoping it would all work out ... like it did in the past.

The only decision I made was not to make any. Bad move. Soon enough, I found myself in deep trouble.

Procrastinating and avoiding my problems didn't make them go away. Instead, they just worsened. Letting others make my decisions for me wasn't working either. How was I going to regain control of my own life? I faced reality and learned how important each choice I make really is. Whether the consequence was a couple of minutes away or a few years in the future, every decision affected me. All I needed to do was think about where each choice was ultimately going to direct me.

I ended up pulling myself together and taking charge, but this time, it was too late. I didn't get accepted into the colleges I wanted. And to make matters worse, I found out that over my summer break, I would have to retake some of the classes I failed during the year. I was bummed, but I sure learned my lesson.

During that summer, Ben often told us how frustrating it was to turn down invitations to parties or road trips. It still annoys him today, because he knows the whole thing could have been avoided in the first place. Remember, ignoring problems is not a formula that makes them go away.

LIVE IT!

Sorry! We don't have an introduction to this section. The waves were too good—way too good for us to be stuck in our hot stuffy rooms typing away. Yeah, we decided to go surfing instead. Hope you don't mind. Hey, what's the big deal? It's only an introduction!

Could you imagine if we really made these excuses? If every time we missed a deadline, we just said, "The computer crashed" or "We were tired" or "We got home too late" or "The dog ate it". If we did, you wouldn't be reading this right now.

The point is, excuses only slow people down. What do they actually produce? Do they bring you fortune? No. Do they bring you results? No. What about happiness? Ahhhh ... here's the trick question: Excuses do bring pleasure; otherwise, no one would make them, right?

Specifically, excuses create "pleasures of the now." Remember them? The problem is, this "happiness" or pleasure wears off ... and fast. Then what are you left with? Nothing! No future and no accomplishments. Now that is not cool.

The problems we try to cover, hide, or forget don't go away or take care of themselves. In fact, in most cases, the situation just worsens with each excuse we add to the pile. And yes, it's sometimes easier to find ways around problems than it is to take care of them. If we make excuses, we become our own worst enemies. We literally defeat ourselves by trying to justify why something didn't work or why something can't be done, instead of figuring out how it CAN be done.

Earlier, we said if you look for excuses—even if you don't look very hard—you WILL find them. It's not like an Easter egg hunt. Your goal should not be to find as many as possible! Instead, let's spend our time looking for opportunities and ways to make things happen instead. Sound good? We know you'll be much happier with results than you would be with a basketful of clever excuses. **If you have a dream ... just live it!**

"Cool Stuff"

THE SOONER YOU ELIMINATE EXCUSES, THE SOONER YOU'LL HAVE THE FUTURE YOU WANT.

One of our dad's friends always—and we mean *always* — gave us a speech about excuses. George must have had Alzheimer's disease (or he thought we did), but his message was important, and it remains branded in our heads. (After all, we heard it so often we've got it memorized!) Let him tell you ...

George: *When I was a boy, I loved boats. My best friend would invite me up to Lake Tahoe with his family, and we'd go boatin' all day, every day. There was nothing I'd rather do. Ever since I was seven years old, I dreamed of owning my own boat, but I didn't actually get it until twenty-seven years later. If I'd only known then what I know now, I would have had the boat and the lifestyle I wanted much sooner. The only thing that was holding me back were* the excuses I kept creating. I always used to tell myself, "I'm too young," "Only rich people have fancy, fast boats," and "Instead of putting a little bit of money aside each week, I'll just wait until I get my promotion at work."

Two decades later, I got sick of not having a boat and realized that my excuses were not getting me any closer to my dream. In fact, they were slowing me waaaay down. I sure got my reality check when I was able to take a step back and recognize that I hadn't attained the things I wanted in life because I was always focusing on the reasons why I could not get them.

KEEP IT CLOSED. When someone annoys you, don't fire back an insult. People often have more respect for those who can keep their cool and their mouth shut. Laurence J. Peter said it perfectly: *"Speak when you're angry and you will make the best speech you'll ever regret."*

I then decided to develop a plan of action. I broke the process into small steps that I had to complete in order to get my boat. Once I mapped things out, I could see exactly what I needed to do and how I was going to get there. For example, I started putting money away each week instead of waiting for a bonus. I took a percentage of my unnecessary expenses (excessive restaurant tabs, nights out, snacks and drinks from vending machines) and put that money aside.

My dream no longer seemed impossible to reach because I now had step-by-step instructions. By changing my mindset as well as my habits, I saw results immediately. As I took action and completed each stage of my plan, I had my boat and many of the other things I wanted in my life, but best of all, I had control of my life.

It was good that George kept his dream, but for many years, he also kept his old ways. He soon realized that a dream followed by excuses will always remain a dream and never come true.

VISION WITHOUT ACTION IS A DAYDREAM.
ACTION WITHOUT VISION IS A NIGHTMARE.

–Japanese Proverb

If George had developed a plan, set priorities, and acted upon them earlier, he would have enjoyed his boat much sooner. He found that the sooner he eliminated his excuses, the sooner he got what he wanted.

SETTING YOUR STAGE FOR LIFE

Sacrifice, sacrifice, sacrifice! Sacrifice all the time! Right?

NO!

To lead a rich and full life, we try to take advantage of every moment we can. After all, we live in the present, right? It's called the present because this time is a valuable gift.

Living IN the moment is fine. Living FOR the moment isn't. There's simply too much future ahead of us! What you do now and the choices you make today are the building blocks that will ultimately shape your future.

The way we act in the moment affects what happens to us later. Often, we create patterns that follow us for the rest of our lives.

Therefore, if you don't like something, the best time to change is now! Why? We forge the majority of our habits early in life. The more time that goes by, the more branded the habits, and the harder they are to change. Things won't improve by themselves. The longer you wait, the harder it becomes to be the person you'd like to be.

This is exactly what Ben experienced. He developed a pattern over the years and learned how to "get by" at school. Over time, it became a habit. Each time he procrastinated or let others make decisions for him, he weakened his future "stage" until it all eventually crumbled right before his eyes. He was lucky he changed it when he did. The more time that passes, the harder it is to change things. Build a sturdy foundation by taking the time to make decisions you'll benefit from one second from now, tomorrow, and the rest of your life.

BECOME AHEAD OF YOUR TIME

What are you thinking of right now?

The best time to get miles ahead of everyone else is while you are still in school. Why? Most people are single-minded. They usually focus on or do one thing at a time, and that "one thing" is usually whatever is right before them at the moment.

Most students who are studying for next week's math test aren't thinking "down the road." They're focused solely on the test and not what comes after that. Develop the habit of asking yourself questions like, "What am I going to do once I graduate?" "How will I make money?" "What do I see myself doing in 10 years?" In other words, lift your eyes and look at the road ahead; think longer term. Many of us are uncomfortable with long-term thinking, because we realize that our answers cannot be absolute; we can't predict the future. True. But by thinking long term, you CAN see opportunities, and you CAN give yourself enough time to make the right decisions to bring your goals in life within your reach.

Fact: Many people don't have a clue about their future because they never seriously think about it. How can you shape the future you want if you don't think about it? You can't. If you don't have direction, events and other people will shape your life for you. Is that what you want? Of course not! So, ask yourself questions about your future, and talk to others who are successful in areas you want to explore later in life. The result: You'll be ahead of most people, and you'll be better prepared—for life!

Never hesitate to ask successful people for their insights, their advice, their "secrets to success." By asking them, you are acknowledging their success, and everyone loves to be acknowledged! As a result, they are always eager to help you.

Tip: Take advantage of potential mentors!

DISCOVER WHAT YOU WANT!

Finding what you want in life instantly empowers you. It gives you a purpose for living and a reason for working hard. It's not uncommon for people to live their entire lives never really knowing what they truly desire. How sad.

This is a problem for two reasons. One: If you go through life not knowing what you want, you won't feel satisfied with what you've accomplished. You run the risk of being unfulfilled, miserable, or depressed. Rotten options! Two: Craving achievement and opportunity is a natural motivator. It motivates you to try your best. A lot of the people we label as "lazy" often just have weak desires. They don't have anything to work toward. They see no personal progress, no reward for their efforts.

Kent: *Obviously, Kyle and I don't always feel motivated and full of creative energy. But we have learned how to change our state of mind. We learned that by concentrating on our desires, we can regain our enthusiasm.*

Example: *We both want to travel around the world, become financially free, and enjoy our career choices. When we feel down or exhausted, we imagine how great it would feel to buy a plane ticket to Fiji and hit the surf or buy our dream cars. This thinking immediately changes our mindset! We get excited and motivated to continue working.*

2K TIP

ON THE BALL. Instead of waiting until you're told to do something, look around. What tasks need to be completed? Be observant, and find things that need to be done before you're asked. This little but remarkable act will always be appreciated—especially by an employer or a parent.

How can you plan and design your future when you don't know what you want? In a way, your desires give you direction, but discovering what you want is the easy part. The challenge is getting what you want. This requires a mix of dreaming, creating realistic goals, and working hard. Use your wants to motivate you to create the right habits now, so you can make your desires a reality.

Tip: Focus on what you want—but also know what you don't want and what you'd like to avoid. Be sure not to focus on them, but know what you don't want so that you can eliminate them from your life.

"Cool Stuff"

WHENEVER YOU CAN ELIMINATE
SOMETHING BAD, IT'S A GOOD THING!

"I PLAN TO ..."

"I plan to get straight A's and go to the college of my choice."

"I plan to own my own company."

"I plan to be the most popular person in the school!"

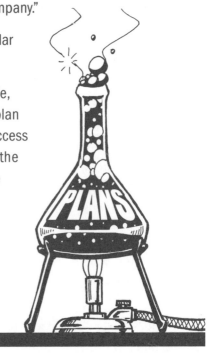

It's difficult, if not impossible, to lead a cheerful life if you don't plan and prepare for happiness and success in the first place. But even the greatest "plans" in the world are worthless if you don't take action to make them happen. Without action, that's all they'll ever be . . . plans. If you believe your line of attack will create the life you want, take action immediately to make it all take shape!

Act immediately, but be patient. It may take weeks, months, or years to see clear, definite results. Unfortunately, there's no magic potion that instantly turns your brilliant ideas into reality.

Most of the time, results depend on small actions or steps. The only way you'll see your plan take shape is by doing what you can right NOW to steer you in the direction you really want to go!

"Cool Stuff"

PLANNING IS ALWAYS IMPORTANT, BUT WITHOUT ACTION, YOU CAN PLAN ON HAVING NOTHING MORE THAN YOU STARTED WITH.

FROM THE MIRROR TO THE STAGE

Our friend Julie found out firsthand how important it is to create plans and follow up on them. Let her tell the story ...

Julie: *I was a dancer at heart. I loved to watch music videos and truly admired the complicated choreographies of a play or a TV show. I would imitate them at home in front of the mirror. One day, my older sister Jessica caught me in the middle of my favorite Britney Spears routine. I felt a little embarrassed but couldn't hide how much I was enjoying myself. To my surprise, Jessica was excited and asked why I wasn't pursuing my passion. It wasn't that I did not want to dance. I did. However, I had no idea how to become a professional dancer.*

I realized I had to have a plan. First, I tried to find out as much as possible about how entertainers got to where they are today. Then I made a list of all the dance studios in my area. I called them and attended the beginners' classes to find which style fit me best. This also gave me a chance to talk to some instructors and get their insights about how to become a dancer. I ended up joining one of the local studios and made friends with a girl who was already in the advanced class. By hanging out and practicing with her, she challenged me further.

As a result, my goal changed. Now, I did not simply want to become a dancer. I wanted to complete all five levels of classes at the studio before my sophomore year in high school so I could perform in the dance company's annual gala. Hopefully, I would eventually get accepted to a college with a strong performing arts program.

I continued to develop my plans and knew exactly what I had to do in order to accomplish my new goals. I practiced hard five days a week, met with my instructors regularly, watched the senior performances, and read as much as I could. It was a very busy time. Two years later, when I was standing on center stage soaking up the applause from the audience, I felt like I was on top of the world. I had done it! But it wasn't until I received my college acceptance letter in the mail that I realized how far away from the mirror I had gone.

"Cool Stuff" FUTURE Builder

1: "What do I want?" List everything you can think of that you want from your life. More friends? Travel around the world? Financial freedom? Cars? Houses? Wrestle a tiger? It is VERY important to know your wants because they will help you to work hard and stay motivated. Why not start now?

_____

_____

_____

_____

_____

2: Pick one ... From your list, pick one item. Remember, you can always get another form at our site (www.coolstuffmedia.com) for each of your other desires!

_____

3: List the steps. For that item, list the steps you must complete to make that desire into a reality. Break the process down into bite-size chunks, into manageable steps. Each time you complete a step, you're already one step closer to your final goal. As you see your progress, you'll feel good about your accomplishment.

a._____

_____

I will complete this step by: _____

b._____

_____

I will complete this step by: _____

c._____

_____

I will complete this step by: _____

d._____

_____

I will complete this step by: _____

4: Which step can you take today? Select one step that will move you closer to your desires.

_____

_____

5: Do it! Take action and reap the rewards!

GET ORGANIZED

When we started writing this book, we had no office, no filing cabinets, and no space! We were going to school full-time and playing sports too. Every second of our time and every square inch of storage had to be used effectively—and they weren't! We couldn't find anything, we kept running out of time, and we felt ridiculously stressed.

It was a nightmare! Something had to change—and fast! To solve our problem, we changed directions. Instead of spending our time researching for the book, we started researching how to get organized.

It was the best time we ever spent! We didn't realize it at the time, but at the pace we were going, it would have taken us two additional lifetimes to finish our book. By spending some time getting organized, we saved countless hours of frustration.

"BUT I'M NOT WRITING A BOOK. WHY SHOULD I GET ORGANIZED?"

Organization relieves stress. When you "get organized," you'll enjoy a variety of benefits:

>> You won't be running around at the last minute like a headless chicken looking for your homework, your keys, your wallet or purse, your ... (*fill in the blank*).
>> You'll know where things are without ripping your room apart.
>> You'll have more space.
>> You'll save time.
>> You'll save money.
>> You'll feel better about yourself!

THE MAGIC NUMBER: 24

We all have the same amount of time in our lives: 24 hours a day. Funny how some people accomplish so much more in their 24 than others! Successful people have learned how to live, play, and work effectively. They have learned how to organize their 24 hours.

Getting organized is one of the best ways to start planning for your future. It can change your life! When you're organized, you're in control. Sound appealing? You'll find that without organization, things are never done on time, perhaps forgotten, or just plain lost forever. Your life will be full of stressful situations you could have avoided. Let's face it: We need to be organized.

Organization is a book in itself. Here, we have only enough space to stress the importance of being effective. Even though you may feel you are getting by "just fine" the way things are right now, life changes. But as school life changes and your work life changes, you might need to fight hard to find spare time. Develop a system that works well for you and discover any method you can to save yourself time, space, and money. Maybe later we'll come out with *"Cool Stuff"* about being organized, but until then, look for ways to improve your efficiency. If we can do it, so can you. Who knows, you could soon have even more spare time to do what you wish.

"I WISH I HAD ..."

During all the interviews we conducted in the process of writing this book, we noticed that a lot of adults began sentences by saying "I wish I had . . ."

"I wish I had started saving money earlier."

"I wish I had known then what I know now!"

"I wish I had a book like this when I was young!" ☺

"I wish I had been told the benefits of planning for the future when I was younger so I could have started earlier."

Most felt like they were one step behind where they wanted to be. They consistently reminded us:

Regret makes a terrible companion.

It's much worse than failure. It sucks your energy and clouds your vision of tomorrow. Even though it is impossible to have a flawless future, you can take what you've learned, put it into practice, and prevent making many decisions you might be disappointed about later.

> "Cool Stuff"
>
> REGRET IS MUCH WORSE THAN FAILURE.

Frank, one of our dad's high school friends, made some decisions when he was younger that he really regrets today. It's very sad to see, but you sure can't go back in time to change things.

Frank: *When I was growing up, I loved cars with a passion. At the beginning of my junior year in high school, I got a job so I could buy a Corvette. I had the hottest ride in the whole school! Everyone loved it. The problem was, I found myself working more and more hours to just to cover my costs. Before long, I was working forty hours a week, trying to go to school, do my homework, and get good grades. I got so caught up in the process of things that I did not realize how ridiculous the situation had become. My social life disappeared. I rarely got to hang out with my friends and go skiing. It seemed the only time I drove my beloved car was when I was going to one of my jobs! It was absurd! There was way too much going on. My hectic schedule seemed to make the next two years fly by.*

When all was said and done, I had missed my high school experience. I never played a sport. And although I graduated, my grades were poor. Was it worth it? No. Can I go back and change it? No. Do I wish I could? Yes. The long-term effects were even greater. My grades prevented me from attending the college of my choice, I started my adult life heavily in debt, and most of my high school memories are of scraping plates and running a dishwasher. So now, when I think of high school, the first thought that comes to mind is, "I wish I had done things differently."

Living with regret is one of the hardest things I've had to deal with.

"BUT WHAT IF ... ?"

"**B**ut what if I lose?"

"But what if he (or she) doesn't like me?"

"But what if they say 'No'?"

Sometimes there just aren't simple answers. If you're having a hard time deciding whether to do something because you might fail, remember that experience can be the best teacher. It may be a difficult teacher because it gives the test first and the lesson afterwards, but you'll definitely learn something.

GOOD JUDGMENT COMES FROM EXPERIENCE, AND EXPERIENCE COMES FROM BAD JUDGMENT.

—Barry LePatner

Don't let lack of experience be a barrier to achievement. If everyone thought that way, we would have no Reactor Board Technology, no Mario & Squeegee Bros., no book called *"Cool Stuff" they should teach in school*. We can't even imagine all the "Cool Stuff" we would have missed out on. To put it simply, if your gut feeling tells you to "go with it," sometimes the best option is just to listen and of course ... take action.

Remember Julie's story? She spent hours in front of the mirror dancing before she realized that she needed to make a decision on what she wanted to do with her passion and talent for dance. Clearly, by realizing that she wanted to become a dancer, Julie hit a fork in the road. She had two choices: She could either continue entertaining herself, and herself only, by doing the one-woman show in front of the mirror, or she could make a plan on how to become a dancer.

2K TIP

LEISURE TIME. Get a hobby. Find something you love to do that will put your mind at ease. Sometimes you just need to get away from it all. While writing this book, we took time to go surfing and enjoy the beach. It's all about balance. Work hard, play hard.

Choosing the mirror had clear advantages: She was comfortable while doing it and risked no criticism. She was not afraid to dance for herself. However, going in front of an audience would bring competition, possibly ridicule. "What if I'm not good enough? What if they don't like me? What if I fail?"

By listening to her gut instinct and following her desires, she avoided the "true failure" of never trying. Of course there were no guarantees that the audience or even her teachers would like her performance, but by trying, she made it possibile to experience success and achieve respect. By trying, she moved from the mirror to the stage. She was happier knowing that she tried versus living a life of "I coulda," "I shoulda," "I woulda." We hope you do the same.

THE WRAP

In order to get the future you want, you need to know what you want. Your desires will give you direction, purpose, and a reason for working hard. By taking charge of your decisions, you will gain control of your life and avoid the "I wish I had ..." syndrome. It's never too soon for you to start designing the future you'd like to have. We hope you've already started by filling out the *"Cool Stuff"* Future Builder; if you have, you're already one step closer to your dreams.

"Cool Stuff"

WHEN YOU HAVE A PLAN OF ATTACK,
YOU INSTANTLY INCREASE YOUR
CHANCES OF SUCCESS.

"Cool Stuff" I need to take note of:

_____

_____

_____

_____

_____

My "To Do" List:

❑ Planning for the future is doing anything I can that I will benefit from one second from now, tomorrow, and the rest of my life.

❑ What I've done and what I'm doing is what matters, not what I *plan to do* or *wish I had done*.

❑ What I do now will affect my future.

❑ If I don't like something, now is the time to change it.

❑ I am prepared for the worst, but I expect the best!

❑ Think about what comes next!

❑ Take action. Otherwise, my plans mean nothing.

❑ Focus on the things I want from life, and work towards getting them.

❑ Get organized so I can be in control of my life!

❑ Creating the future I want is easy ... as long as I start thinking about it now!

The Wrap

15

In the end,
it is up
to you.

YOUR FUTURE

> IF YOU CONTINUE TO DO WHAT YOU'VE ALWAYS DONE, AND YOU CONTINUE TO THINK AS YOU'VE ALWAYS THOUGHT, YOU WILL CONTINUE TO GET WHAT YOU'VE ALWAYS GOTTEN.
>
> — *Unknown*

Picture this: The year is 2055. Kent and Kyle are slumping in their rockers, doing what they do best ... reminiscing about the past.

Kyle: *Hey, Kent! I been thinkin'. Remember that time you said something ridiculous about writing a book together? I think of that every once in a while, and I just laugh. And we were only teenagers!*

Kent: *Why? What's so funny? We could have written that book...*

One thing for sure: When we're older, we will NOT regret "the Cool Stuff book we never wrote." For over three years, we worked on this book—writing, reading, researching, and of course, rewriting and rewriting and then rewriting again. Talk about a lot of work!

We have made a lot of mistakes, but we KNOW we did one thing right: We followed our dreams. We followed through until we completed our goal. Sure, there were times when it felt like we were getting nowhere. Our focus and our determination were tested all of the time, but every time we were tested we remembered this little (but important) lesson:

And the sum of all our "small steps" brought us to the end of our three-year-long journey. We achieved our objective and finished this book while we were both in our teens. You may not want to write a book, but hey, your goals and aspirations will become possible the minute you believe and commit to them.

No, creating the life you want is not going to be a "piece of cake." However, it's A LOT easier to head in the right direction now rather than trying to correct your course later. Like we said earlier, it's easy to find reasons not to do something. You don't even need to look for them—excuses will always be there.

Take action! It's simple: If you do nothing, you'll get nothing. If you wait for other people to make decisions for you, you will get results (but not necessarily the ones you want).

Your future lies in your hands—no one else's. Advice will always be there for you to take or leave, but in the end, only *your* decisions matter. Shape your life by making the right ones. Finish what you start, and be the person you know you can be.

TWENTY YEARS FROM NOW YOU WILL BE
MORE DISAPPOINTED BY THE THINGS
THAT YOU DIDN'T DO THAN BY THE ONES
THAT YOU DID DO. SO THROW OFF THE
BOWLINES. SAIL AWAY FROM THE SAFE
HARBOR. CATCH THE TRADE WINDS IN
YOUR SAILS. EXPLORE. DREAM. DISCOVER.

— *Mark Twain*

In the year 2055, what will YOU be saying to your brother, your best friend, your grandkids? Hmmm ...

About the Authors

We were born in San Jose, which is in Northern California. Our first school, a public elementary school in the hills of Cupertino, had fewer than forty students. At ages nine and ten, our lives took a seriously weird turn. We thought, "Our parents must be crazy!" They dragged us halfway around the world to continue our lives in New Zealand! (Yes, it's the country next to Australia.)

In New Zealand, we learned to surf, dive, snowboard, wakeboard, and play the national game, rugby. It seemed we were never bored. If we weren't building downhill mountain bike courses and BMX tracks, then we were managing our surf/skate/skimboard business or working at the local surf club or playing sports. We became lifeguards, and both of us patrolled and surfed the local beaches. Our patrol area included a nudist beach, inhabited mostly by old, flabby people—we still have nightmares.

Our lives were always changing. Every day was completely different, and our commitment to sports only made things more complicated. In total, we attended five different high schools, lived in eight different houses, and resided in six different cities. It was exciting, but sometimes it was tough too. "Character building," some would say. One thing is for sure: We grew up looking at life a little bit differently ...

Kyle

Kent

We've been lucky enough to travel to many countries, live overseas, have extraordinary experiences, and receive a lot of help from smart, successful people (including our parents). What this has really taught us is where to go, who to approach, and what to ask to get the answers we need.

In this book, our goal is to provide the fundamentals we all need to cruise into the "real world" with styyyyyle!

BECOME PART
OF THIS BOOK

WAIT! DON'T PUT THIS BOOK DOWN!

We want to make this book the best it can be! To do that, we need YOU. Now that you have finished this book, check out our site to win some *"Cool Stuff"*:

WWW.COOLSTUFFMEDIA.COM

Once there, you'll have an opportunity to tell us what you like, don't like, and want to see more of. If you have a story that you think would fit into this book, be sure to let us know because your idea might get published!

Don't be a stranger ... check our website every once in a while to see what we're up to and what Cool Books are coming up next. Let us know what you would like to hear more about. Who knows ... maybe we'll write a book about that too!

We hope you enjoyed this book.

Your friends,

Kent & Ryle

ABOUT THE ARTIST

Born in Iowa, Shawn King is a self-taught artist who has a degree in computer science, graphics, and web design. He enjoys doing freelance work and specializes in black-and-white illustrations and computer coloring. He has been published by independent comic companies and has done layouts and logo design work for local businesses.

LOOKING BACK...
PHOTOS FROM OUR SCRAPBOOK

KENT'S ROOM ... A.K.A OUR OFFICE/RESEARCH CENTER/
INTERNATIONAL HEADQUATERS ... IN THE EARLY STAGES OF
WRITING THE BOOK. AT A NEAR 103 DEGREES IT WAS GREAT
TO CELEBRATE THE COMPLETION OF CHAPTER ONE.

THE DESIGN CREW AT 9:15PM   THE DESIGN CREW AT
                             2:10AM

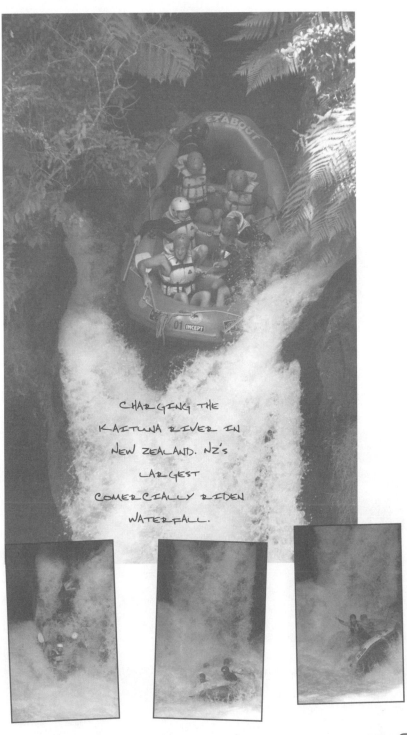

CHARGING THE
KAITUNA RIVER IN
NEW ZEALAND. NZ's
LARGEST
COMERCIALLY RIDEN
WATERFALL.

OUR "OUTSIDE" OFFICE ...

HOW WE SKIMBOARD IN AUSTRALIA ...

THE DISMOUNT
NEEDS
IMPROVEMENT

SNACKS IN CHINA ...
WHAT IS THIS!?

BIG TROUBLE IN
LITTLE CHINA

BIKER
GANG
ON A
BUDGET

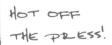

HOT OFF
THE PRESS!

OUR FIRST ARTICLE.
WAIT ... DOES THIS MEAN
WE'RE FAMOUS NOW?

KENT INVADING INTERNATIONAL AIR
SPACE ... YEAH RIGHT!

KYLE'S COFFEE BREAK.
SKIMBOARDING IN SAN CLEMENTE, CA

IT WAS COOL TO
SEE OUR REACTOR
SKATEBOARDS IN
STORES

ONE OF OUR
REACTOR
SKIMBOARDS

MATAKANA ISLAND,
NEW ZEALAND

SURF SAFARIS

CRUSIN' THE
TROPICS

SKY TOWER. NEW ZEALAND'S HIGHEST JUMP — 192 METERS (624 FT).

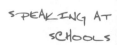

SPEAKING AT SCHOOLS

PROM, 70'S STYLE.
"IF WE LOOK SO GOOD, WHERE ARE OUR DATES?"

... AFTER SELLING OUR POSSESSIONS TO FUND OUR BOOK

I CAN'T BELIEVE WE GOT THESE GLASSES FOR HALF PRICE!

THE MARIO AND SQUEEGEE BROS. AT WORK

OUR DOGS,
TEAL AND CODY

OUR GREATEST INSPIRATION